P9-CBH-565

BUSH PILOTS

Legends *of the* Old & Bold

by Bob Cary & Jack Hautala

ADVENTURE PUBLICATIONS, INC.
CAMBRIDGE, MN

Cover and interior design by Jonathan Norberg
Photos contributed by Bob Cary and Jack Hautala
Special thanks to Eric Helmuth for recording and mastering the audio CD

Second Printing
Copyright 2003 by Bob Cary and Jack Hautala
Published by Adventure Publications, Inc.
820 Cleveland Street South
Cambridge, MN 55008
1-800-678-7006
ISBN: 1-59193-010-3
Printed in the USA

BUSH PILOTS: LEGENDS OF THE OLD & BOLD

INTRO

It did not take long for early pilots to figure out that an airplane could be put on some kind of floats and operated off water. By the 1920s, aluminum planes and aluminum floats were connected and the era of bush pilots began. "Bush" refers to the Canadian word for the vast forest and lake country that extends from northern Minnesota to the Arctic.

The wild half-century, from 1930 into the 1970s, was the golden age of floatplane flying in Ely, Minnesota. There were more floatplanes and bush pilots operating out of Ely than anywhere else in North America. They hauled thousands of fishermen into seldom-fished lakes inside the roadless wilderness, lakes teeming with walleyes, lake trout, northern pike and bass. Hunters, canoe parties and remote resorts also came to rely on the bush pilots.

These enterprises eventually came into conflict with the paddle-only wilderness people, and a half century of political conflict existed side-by-side with the floatplanes. Eventually, floatplanes were eliminated from the Ely area except for U.S. Forest Service patrol craft. Some of the bush pilots headed north to Alaska and continued flying. Some went elsewhere looking for wheel plane work. Some quit flying. But while the floatplane era lasted in Ely, it generated some of the most exciting, crazy, funny and sometimes tragic incidents in the history of the Northland. It was the privilege and luck of the authors to have been a part of it and to have experienced it. It is our hope that the readers can share with us some of that lore and excitement.

Each year, thousands of enterprising individuals take flying lessons and receive private pilot's ratings. A few hundred take lessons on water and learn to fly on floats. Some of these take advanced training and acquire a commercial floatplane license. And a very few, if they fly long enough and live long enough, gain the skills to fly the wilderness in any season, in any weather, with no more than a map, the ability to read the terrain, and the knowledge of how to survive if forced down. There are a good number of pilots who fly the bush, but there are only a few genuine bush pilots.

4

Hanging on the wooden wall of the old Wilderness Wings Airways operations shack was a large sign that read:

There are old pilots
And there are bold pilots,
but there are no old, bold pilots

The point being that skilled, but cautious pilots don't take chances and thus live a long time. And there is considerable truth in this. But of all the veteran bush pilots the authors have known, every one, at various times, simply had to be bold to survive. Hurtling through a hammering rain, banging sleet, blinding snow, pea soup fog or pitch black night with nothing below but trees, rocks and water, is no place for indecision or faintness of heart. This book is mainly about the old and the bold, those fliers of the wilderness who play the odds with consummate skill and iron nerve. It has been a privilege to know and fly with so many of them.

Switch on! Contact! Let's get 'er rolling!

THE REAL OLD DAYS

"I guess the first airplane I ever saw was in the 1920s..."

LINDBERGH SYNDROME

BY BOB CARY

$\mathcal{Y}$oung people growing up in the United States today have no idea of the impact Charles Lindbergh had on American youth in the 1920s and 1930s. Lindbergh, who grew up in Little Falls, Minnesota, had an early interest in aviation and became a pilot flying mail for the U.S. Air Service in 1926. In 1927, he set out to win the $25,000 Ortieg prize offered to the first flier to cross the Atlantic Ocean solo. On May 20, 1927, he took off from Roosevelt Field, Long Island, and landed 33½ hours later at Le Bourget Field, Paris, becoming an overnight world sensation. "Lindy" was instantly a household name, the idol of every young man with a drop of adventure in his blood.

Ely pilot Bill Rom, who later became the most successful canoe outfitter in North America, recalls he was nine years old when Lindbergh made his famous flight.

"My grade school friend Louis Pechaver and I ran up and down the alley in back of our house, holding our arms extended and yelling our best imitations of the Wright J-5 radial engine that powered Lindy's aircraft. Louis was so busy at this, he was nicknamed 'Lindy Louie' by the neighbors, but his flying career never progressed beyond this stage. We had another friend, Merlin Krause, who fashioned a pair of wings out of cardboard, climbed to the roof of his back porch, tied on the wings and jumped off. He broke both wrists on his landing.

"I guess the first airplane I ever saw was in the 1920s when a pilot with a two-place open cockpit wheel plane was taking passengers up for five-minute flights off a plowed strip on the ice of Brisson's Bay at Shagawa Lake. The charge was five dollars, but it might just as well have been five hundred because I didn't have a nickel. Only a few well-off businessmen made the flight. They wore leather helmets and heavy coats against the cold wind.

"I took my first flight in 1932 with Millard Whittig of Hibbing who was barnstorming out of the first Ely Airport in a Curtiss Robin at 50 cents a head. Millard later fatally crashed a Cessna 195 with his two brothers in a snowstorm."

Like all the old northern Minnesota pilots, Bill remembers the first Ely Airport located just south of the cemetery in the area now occupied by the Ely softball complex. A high power line was on the east and city homes to the west. On the south was Highway 1 and another power line. "You were boxed in with hazards in every direction," Rom recalls. "The pilots flying in said the cemetery was at least located in a handy place."

Ely made front page news in 1933 with the dedication of the airport and an air show featuring stunt pilot Malcolm Dunlop from Duluth. Dunlop came roaring across the field in a spectacular barrel roll, hooked a wing and crashed.

The crowd watched in horror as the wood-and-fabric plane exploded in flames with the pilot trapped inside. Dunlop Field was named for him.

A Cessna 185 from the Ely seaplane base

Not long after the field was opened, a barnstorming pilot with a big Ford Tri-Motor came in to conduct excursion trips. Nobody told him the field was exceptionally short. While he landed ok, he found it impossible to take off. After some study and discussion with the city fathers, the plane was towed with a tractor around the east side of Ely to Camp Street; the street was cleared of traffic and the pilot took off with the Ford Tri-Motor.

"In January, 1935," Rom recalls, "Jiggs Hegfors, Tony Slogar, an official from the Skelly Oil Company and I pitched in five bucks apiece to hire Oscar Ringnell to take us winter fishing on Lake Gabimichigami. We caught a couple of trout but hit a snowstorm on the way home. Oscar put the Curtiss Robin down at Bill Berglund's Resort on Knife Lake (later home of Root Beer Lady, Dorothy Molter). Tony had a gallon of wine and a case of beer along, which made the time go faster.

"Oscar had a well-earned reputation for hard drinking. He kept sipping wine and looking out the cabin window. At length, he said he could see just fine through the snow and was ready to take off, although none of the others could see the other side of the lake.

"Half-soused Oscar got us safely home," Bill recalled. "They say Oscar had to be lifted out of the plane more than once after executing a perfect landing while under the influence. He could drink and he could fly, but sometimes he just couldn't walk."

One thing about Ringnell, however; he always dressed well. Photos taken of him in his flying days showed him with a shirt, tie, jacket, suitcoat, polished oxfords and a fedora. Once he was stranded in the wilderness at Gabimichigami Lake for three days with three men when the plane's engine wouldn't start. It was 30 below and they had no camping gear or sleeping bags and two of the men had only street shoes. They huddled up inside the plane but eventually wound up at the Shipman Hospital with frostbitten feet. Oscar probably saved their lives by heating rocks in the fire and carrying them to the plane in his engine cover. He was irritated, however, with the fact that he burned a couple of holes in the cover. It was one he had stolen off Wiley Post's Winnie Mae some time before Post crashed in the tundra at Pt. Barrow, Alaska, with humorist Will Rogers.

"There were a lot of crack-ups in the old and not so 'good old' days," Bill recalls. "Jesse Swanson splattered his Curtiss Robin all over the ice when he was buzzing his girlfriend's mother's house on Burntside Lake. Luckily, Jesse and his passenger Louis Palcher walked away from the wreck.

"I was the first one on the scene after Paul Erzar spun in near

Voody's Bay on White Iron Lake. He had a 26-year-old relative from California up with him and was stunting in an Aeronca Champ. No one saw him go down but residents reported hearing the crash. Early the next day, State Inspector Havley, who happened to be in Ely at the time, asked Forest Service pilot Chick Beel and I if we would conduct a search. Chick located the wreckage and my job was to land and walk to the site where I found both men dead.

"Paul had crawled through the broken windshield and was lying underneath the tail with his head resting on his arm. Had he been found right after the crash, he might have made it. The passenger, dead in the back seat, had a leg severed at the ankle and a slash across his forehead. His foot was still in his tennis shoe when I picked it up."

Bill took flying lessons at the Wold Chamberlain Field in Minneapolis in 1939. Fellow students were deer hunting buddies Ed Erler and Ten Finholt. The latter went on to become a Northwest Airlines pilot. Bill tried to get assigned to the Navy Flying School at Pensacola, Florida, in 1940, but couldn't pass the eye exam. He ended up in the Navy and served on the carrier *Bismarck Sea*, transferring to another ship just before the carrier was destroyed by Kamikaze planes off Iwo Jima. Bill served on the U.S.S. *Maryland* and flew sometimes with Ray Glumack, who piloted a Navy observation plane off the ship. Glumack later was part owner of the Eveleth Airport and then became Director of the Metropolitan Airport Commission for the Minneapolis-St. Paul International Airport.

"After the war I resumed flying under the G.I. Bill and the Leithold Seaplane Base, getting my private sea and land rating. Bill Leithold was one of the most experienced and efficient instructors in this area. He was patient in taxiing, always going to the far shore before a takeoff and leaving no unused air strip behind. Leithold flew for Northwest Airlines but preferred flying in the bush and gave up a lucrative job just to fly fishermen into the wilderness. He developed the Leithold Seaplane Base at Sandy Point on Shagawa Lake along with Waino Wirtanen, Holden Guldberg and Jack Isaac, a retired Navy pilot. They had about a dozen planes, some used in their flying school."

Waino Wirtanen had flown extensively with the Wein brothers who started in Cook, Minnesota, then moved to Alaska and set up

Wein Alaska Airways, which eventually became the present Air Alaska.

"Flying must be in our family blood," Bill continued, "because all of the family flew, including my wife Barbara, sons Bill Jr. and Larry, and daughter Becky who took a prize in aerobatic stunt flying at an Eveleth air show. Larry went on to fly in Alaska and is currently flying bush in the Ely area and to our camp at Harris Lake in Canada."

One fall, Larry flew in with his Labrador retriever to the family operation on Harris Lake to shut down for the winter. While busy draining pipes, he heard a howl from the Labrador, and ran around the corner of the cabin to see a bear had the dog by the head. Larry rushed up and put a boot into the ribs of the bear, which promptly turned on him, knocked him down and lacerated his leg. Larry and the dog managed to make it back to the float-plane and flew to Ely where his cuts were sewn up.

Bill Rom didn't fly commercially for air services but used his plane for emergencies and for locating and bringing out canoe paddlers who had difficulty. He assisted in bringing out several drowning victims and helped locate a number of plane crashes in the wilderness. He has also been active in national conservation programs, among them the creation of Voyageur's National Park.

"When the park was first projected, a number of national conservation figures came up to fly over and inspect the Kabetogema Peninsula. My old friend Francis Einerson, who operated the International Falls Airport, told me he received a phone call one day from a fellow who wanted to rent a two-place airplane to fly over the proposed park area. Einerson asked what the caller's name was and the man answered 'Charles Lindbergh.'

"Einerson laughed and said, 'Yeah, and I'm General Jimmy Doolittle.'

"A few days later, the men arrived to fly over the park and Einerson was startled to see one of them was unmistakably Charles Lindbergh, who later was instrumental in getting the park created."

THE FEDS on FLOATS

BY BOB CARY

C. E. "Dusty" Rhodes was a flamboyant figure, the first seaplane pilot the U.S. Forest Service hired to patrol the Superior National Forest in 1929. Oddly enough, it was that same Forest Service that put Rhodes out of the private flying business in the 1950s with the air ban.

Someone in the USFS hierarchy figured out that one airplane and one pilot could patrol a larger area, pinpoint more fires and provide more assistance to wilderness travelers than a dozen forest rangers sitting all day alone in steel fire towers scattered across hundreds of square miles of woods. In addition, the aircraft gave fire crews mobility. One other benefit was that they also provided a few government V.I.P.s quick access to some of the best sport fishing in North America. But that aspect never interfered with the mission of the Feds on Floats.

At the same time Rhodes was hired, Scenic Airways was formed in Ely by Herb Kurvinen and T. J. Somero. At that time there were no restrictions on flying into the canoe country. Somero and Kurvinen began hauling fishermen to remote lakes and also encouraged the Forest Service to develop more floatplane use. They teamed up with a pilot named Dutch Fuller who was flying commercially. While they were usually paid for government work, they often volunteered their services to fly in personnel and equipment to fight fires and supply timber crews. The mobility afforded by seaplanes was immediately apparent in an area where roads were few but lakes abundant.

In 1935, much of the forest air patrol work was under contract, but most fires were still being fought by crews sent in by watercraft and on foot. There was a stiff cost involved in having private planes and pilots paid on "standby." The first contract seaplane in

13

general use was an amphibian, which presented problems in landing along the granite shores of many lakes. In 1936, the Forest Service replaced the amphibian with a floatplane—a four-place, 220-horsepower Stinson that provided good service and boosted the popularity of floatplane use.

U.S. Forest Service pilot Dean Lee with snorkel used on Beavers for fire fighting

The government had no maintenance facilities for the Stinson, which was simply anchored in the bay; but in 1941, a 60-by-60-foot hangar and a dock were under construction, later expanded to the current docks and spacious hangar.

An additional seaplane, a two-place, 65-horsepower Cub Coupe J-4, was purchased and put in operation. The Stinson only lasted to June of 1943 when it was totaled in a crash. In 1944, the USFS purchased a 10-place, 600-horsepower DeHaviland Norseman, followed by a 215-horsepower, four-place Seabee in 1948. The Seabee presented problems and was replaced the following year with a four-place, 165-horsepower Stinson.

The first seven-passenger DeHaviland Beaver with a 450-horse Pratt and Whitney power unit was put into service in 1956, followed by several more. The Superior National Forest currently owns four Beavers, all of which are nearly 50 years old, but all maintained in excellent condition and flying regular patrols.

During the time of switch over to Beavers, pilot Chick Beel and some of the other airmen involved in firefighting had been experimenting with various types of water pickup, which evolved to the current 125-gallon belly tank filled by a snorkel tube. This allowed the seaplane to land, skim the surface of a lake and take off with a full load to drop on the flames. When this device was perfected, newspaper reporters were contacted around the Midwest and invited to come up and see the process. Thus it was that this writer left his home base in Chicago and drove to Ely for a demonstration. The pilot was instructed to come over low and close to the dock so the reporter could take a photo of the water being released. The pilot obligingly brought the Beaver in low and as the camera shutter clicked, 125 gallons of water smacked me dead center. There was no question but what any of the Kawishiwi District pilots could target any fire they wished to attack. Eventually, the entire USFS adopted Beel's design, which is now in use on all forests and provided considerable deterrent in the terrible fire years of 2001 and 2002.

C. E. "Dusty" Rhodes

When the tanker system was being developed, there was also progress being made in adding fire retardant chemicals to the water that would have a further depressing effect on forest fires. Walt Newman remembers when one such test was being conducted for the benefit of government dignitaries alongside a lake where picnic tables were set up with a fine lunch. The pilot, wishing to impress the viewers with his skill, came in low and close to release his load of chemically-treated water. Unfortunately, he hit the picnic table. "We had white stuff all over the food, in the mustard and everywhere," Newman said.

Fire patrol could take some odd twists. Waino Wirtanen, who flew for a number of years, recalled an incident in the 1960s with a cantankerous old woods character named Sumner Purvis who dwelt in a lakeside homestead between Ely and Tower. Purvis, a Spanish-American War veteran, lived to be over 100 and eked out a living from a large garden and what he could glean from the forest. He had developed an antagonistic attitude toward loggers whom he regarded as destroyers of his beloved woods. One summer, there were a number of reports of fires in slash piles following timber cutting near Purvis' domain.

Wirtanen was flying patrol and spotted several slash piles aflame. He picked up a load of water and dropped it on one fire, then spotted Purvis darting out of the woods to set fire to another slash pile. Wirtanen swooped down on a lake, picked up another load of water and flew back to where Purvis was setting the blazes. "I targeted him with the next load of water, hit him dead center and he quit starting fires," Waino said.

The current USFS roster consists of Wayne Erickson, Dean Lee and Pat Loe. Unlike earlier U.S. Forest Service pilots who needed merely to be able to fly, these pilots have depth of experience and training.

Chief Pilot Wayne Erickson has been flying since 1974. He flew commercially for Bohman Airways out of International Falls, then logged eight years in Alaska. His work there involved flying research teams and equipment out on the Arctic ice pack, handling planes up to DC-3 amphibs. In 1989 he came back to Minnesota to fly with the Superior National Forest and plans to finish his career at that post.

Dean Lee grew up in Maine with an avid interest in flying. He attended the Florida Institute of Technology, learned airplane mechanics and took pilot training. After completing school, he returned to Maine and served on the Allagash Forest, flying fire patrol and also ferrying canoes and people taking trips on Maine rivers. He later flew out of Connecticut with passenger trips to New York City on amphibs that could land on either land or water. He returned to Maine and spent several years in home construction, but flying was in his blood. He hired on to fly floatplanes for oil companies in Louisiana servicing water-oriented oil rigs. In 1984 he returned to Maine; both flying and applying his knowledge of airplane mechanics. Like the others, he next flew a variety of planes in Alaska including DC-3s on floats, then signed on in 1991 with the Forest Service at Ely.

U.S. Forest Service pilots Wayne Erickson and Pat Loe

Pat Loe is a Minnesota native, went through the public school system, learned aviation at St. Cloud State, earned his multi-engine rating and flew for commuter airlines in Minnesota. He went to work for the Forest Service in Alaska, flying Beavers. He transferred to Minnesota's Superior National Forest in 1998 to fly more Beavers out of the Ely base. Pat served a hitch as a U.S. Army paratrooper and found his hand-to-hand combat training useful one night a few weeks before Christmas, 2002. He was awakened in the middle of the night by sounds of a prowler attempting to burglarize his garage. Slamming on a pair of boots and rushing through the snow in his pajamas, he cornered the thief who snarled that he was armed with a knife. Those were the last words the burglar got out before Loe flattened him, then dragged him into the house, and phoned the police. Next day, the street comment around Ely was that "the burglar picked the wrong garage to burgle."

Today, the Forest Service fleet, in addition to patrolling and fighting fires, also acts as an emergency rescue unit. In recent years, USFS floatplanes have conducted from 10 to 15 missions each summer to bring out injured or sick canoe campers from the wilderness. They have also been valuable in finding campers reported lost within the Boundary Waters.

Erickson, Lee and Loe comprised the staff when the July 4, 1999, storm ripped through the Boundary Waters wilderness, leveling timber from Ely to Gunflint, burying the portage trails with logs and brush and marooning hundreds of canoe campers. The three pilots flew almost nonstop for two days, dropping in on campsites to check on stranded paddlers and flying out injured campers. In some cases they had to cut their way through downed trees to reach the people. Although there were 20 injuries, some severe, prompt rescue efforts averted possible fatalities. Despite the hazards of landing in lakes filled with brush and floating logs, these skilled pilots logged not a single accident.

Indeed, there have been relatively few crashes since the Feds began flying on the Superior in 1929 and not a single fatality among the USFS pilots.

With the air ban going into effect in 1954 and eventual elimination of private flying in the wilderness, the work of the Forest Service pilots has become more important as they assumed rescue missions formerly assigned to private or state fliers. Fire patrols have been supplemented by airborne fire fighting units with equipment and personnel taken directly to fires or to lakes from which fires can be reached on foot. Coupled with the snorkel water tanker system, forest fire loss has been kept to a minimum.

The roster of pilots who served the federal operation reads like a "Who's Who" in floatplane lore. Dusty Rhodes, mentioned earlier as the first USFS pilot on the Superior Forest, also flew for commercial operators until the air ban came into effect. Rhodes eventually gave up floatplane flying and the last anyone knew, was operating a wild animal farm as a tourist attraction in Wisconsin. Other pilots, some on contract, included: Herb Kurvinen, T. J. Somero, T. L. "Dutch" Fuller, Milt Nelson, Eric Berg, Hilding Anderson, Ernest "Hoot" Hautala, William Leithold, Merle

Moltrup, Chick Beel, Walt Newman, Waino Wirtanen, Steve Gheen, Carlo Palombi and Roy Hangartner. Since 1952, no one but government pilots have ventured into the Boundary Waters except for special emergencies.

While there are still a few private floatplanes operating on the rim of the Superior National Forest, all of the low level patrols, fire fighting or rescue missions into the wilderness are conducted by uniformed Forest Service pilots in well-maintained DeHaviland Beavers. This is a small but proud cadre of bush pilots, confident of their ability and secure in their knowledge of the aircraft they fly.

U.S. Forest Service Beaver docked

THE MAN THEY CALLED "CHICK"

BY BOB CARY

$\mathcal{S}$ome people get the mistaken idea that bush pilot "Chick" Beel may have gotten his nickname from "chicken." But chicken he is not. There is no more gutsy guy around the north country. He is a little stooped and weathered now, partially from the ravages of cancer. Indeed, he laughs sardonically when pointing out that something like six years ago, doctors gave him no more than two years to live. Chick fooled them all, like he's fooled fate for much of his 76 years, a lot of that time in the air in some tight situations over fog-shrouded pine trees and rock ridges.

The Beel family moved into a new Ely mining development in 1919 called Pioneer Location or Calumet Location, depending on who you talk to or how well their memory is functioning. Chick was born there in 1924. He gives credit for his early interest in flying to his boyhood home because he lived just two blocks from the Sandy Point Seaplane Base that housed Scenic Airways, owned by Herb Kurvinen and T. J. Somero. Chick saw the wreck when Dutch Fuller stuck his plane into a backyard at Chandler Location and he also saw Duluth stunt pilot Malcolm Dunlop crash at the opening of the original Ely Airport. He was on hand when the Ford Tri-Motor flew off Camp Street after it was towed there with a tractor because the Ely air strip was too short for takeoff for a plane of that size.

He spent his early years fishing and hunting (like most of the boys growing up in that area), attended public school, went into the military service in 1942 and got out in 1946 with a wife, daughter and a burning desire to fly.

Sandy Point was then owned by Bill Leithold who got his start in Chicago in 1927. Leithold hooked up with Holden Guldberg, Jack Isaac and Waino Wirtanen to operate a wilderness fly-in service and a floatplane school. The G.I. Education Bill, provided by the U.S. Congress to help returning WWII servicemen get a start in civilian life, had a section that allowed veterans to take flying lessons at government expense. More than 40 men from Ely signed up at the Leithold base, including Chick. At the time he enrolled under the G.I. Bill he had accumulated 4 hours and 15 minutes of dual flight time out of his own pocket. Until the government program started, becoming a pilot seemed some distance away.

He was such a quick study, finishing the course and exhibiting sufficient skills, that Leithold hired him to fly. Chick began accumulating hundreds of hours and absorbing valuable flight knowledge. Eventually he would fly for all the major Ely seaplane bases including Elwyn West and Pat Magie and also flew regularly for the U.S. Forest Service.

He recalls Elwyn West, a superb pilot from Waupaca, Wisconsin, who periodically exhibited a short fuse. Once, West got into a confrontation with an official from the FAA that ended in a fist fight with West flattening the government man. He had his flying license revoked for assaulting a federal officer, but eventually got it reinstated following intervention from Wisconsin Senator Robert LaFollette, who knew West when he was flying out of Waupaca.

Flying bush in the early days, Chick recalls, was sometimes hairy. "We flew in all kinds of conditions, some of the worst in snow and fog. There were times when I wished I was somewhere else other than in the air, but I always got down OK."

Learning the tricks of flying in winter conditions was something gleaned from the old-timers. "Snow on a lake could hide what we called 'a sucker hole,'" Chick said, "which usually involved pockets of slush. The nice thing about a Beaver was that you could fly it slow. You could land it easily without power if you had to."

When flying for Leithold, Chick was sometimes obliged to fly out the mortal remains of someone who either died of a heart attack or drowned in a canoe accident. "Funny thing," he notes, "you can easily pick up a guy who weighs 150 pounds alive, but when he's dead he feels like 300 pounds."

One matter Chick continually refers to was paying attention to details. He always checked and rechecked his controls, fuel and ignition. In that respect, he was like a lot of young pilots who eventually got to be old pilots. "You had to pay attention," he recalled. And then went on to tell about a pilot coming into the airport who ran into a flock of geese. "He got so distracted by the birds, he forgot to put his wheels down. That caused a mess."

One of the planes Chick particularly liked was the Norseman. "It vibrated a lot, but it had plenty of power. The trouble was, it was big and flew a lot of cargo. When you flew the Norseman you became a stevedore, moving heavy loads in and out."

He likes to classify the Norseman as an "85 plane." That is, it would "take off at 85 miles per hour, fly at 85 miles per hour and would also stall at 85, if the pilot wasn't taking care of business."

When Chick flew for Pat Magie, there were some flights in extremely poor weather. "Sometimes we flew with a half mile visibility on the ground, which meant less than half that when you were in the air. Under those conditions, trees are moving fast as they come whistling at you. Sometimes there was a lot of fog hanging over the snow, which made it difficult to pick out the shoreline of a lake. We sometimes came in 'dragging our feet' to get down as slow as possible. We would make our best guess as to where the main part of a frozen lake was, where the islands were, and at the last moment it was do or die."

Chick thought for a moment. "I never did care much for that 'die' part. Flying into the dark was another hazard. One thing you learn about flying late in the day: If you come in facing where the sun went down, you have more twilight visibility than flying into the dark with sundown at your back."

When Chick was operating for the Forest Service he flew numerous fire patrols. He and Milt Nelson developed the snorkel system, the fire-fighting tanker system that allowed a pilot to come in on his floats, skim the lake surface, pick up a load of water and fly back to a forest fire without stopping. Using his invention, Chick and Milt flew a number of fire-fighting missions, running water shuttles from nearby lakes to fires.

Once he spotted a pair of firefighters who were cut off by the flames near the Echo Trail and had made their way to a beach on a small lake. Chick managed to get down through the smoke and picked up the men, apologizing: "Sorry I'm late. One of our seaplanes is down with engine trouble."

Once he came in from Ramshead Lake at night in a fog, looking for Shagawa Lake. He could vaguely make out the lights of Ely below but had no fix on the shoreline. He gave it his best guess and started to let down, "dragging his feet."

"I greased her in," Chick said, coolly. "My only concern was that somebody might be running around out in the dark in a boat. Didn't happen. We got to the base OK.

"One time Bill Leithold came in with his Stinson at night and cut a boat in half. Luckily, the guy driving the boat jumped out just before the plane hit."

One Forest Service patrol Chick enjoyed was flying the annual state moose survey with DNR Game Wardens Bob Hodge and Bob Jacobsen. "We flew grids, counting the numbers of cows and bulls in each grid.

"Jacobsen had a sharp eye for spotting moose, almost uncanny at sorting out bulls and cows in the balsam brush. Once somebody asked Jake how he could be so sure which was a cow and which was a bull. 'I have Chick fly real low, right between their legs, and I look up to see,' Jake said with a grin."

In reality, they did fly very low, and close to stalling speed, often less than 800 feet in the air, which is exceedingly tight if engine trouble should occur. It is also an altitude where the pilot has no recovery room in the event of a stall. They never lost a ship nor a pilot on the moose surveys.

There was always some comment among old time pilots that the Forest Service hired Chick to fly for the government just to make him "legal." There were stories that Chick flew trappers into wilderness areas off-limits to trapping. Chick just laughs at that one, although he allows there were pilots who sometimes fudged the rules to make a little pocket cash. While such rumors persisted about Chick, he was never arrested, never convicted for any illegal activity. Which, some say, is either a testament to his honesty or a tribute to his superior flying skill.

"One of the things that gave us a pain at the Forest Service base was the occasional government big shot who came in from Washington, D. C., on an inspection trip. Basically, they were looking for something negative they could report, and we didn't care much for them. Most of them didn't know anything about floatplanes, either."

Once a nosy inspector came poking around the hangar, snooping inside the planes, asking Chick a continual barrage of questions about just exactly what the pilots did and how they did it. "I told the guy we did a lot of on-the-water practice to sharpen our skills and asked if he would like to see a demonstration. He climbed in the Beaver and I took him for a wild ride around the islands on Shagawa Lake, first up on one float then on the other. After a few minutes of zigzagging around I thought he looked properly impressed and I raced back to the dock. He jumped out of the Beaver, ran to his car and vanished. Never saw him again."

Chick flew for the Forest Service until 1976, then came out of retirement when needed for a few flights in 1977 and 1978. Because he was afraid a lot of the floatplane history of the area would be lost if he died, he began writing a series of weekly articles for the Ely Echo Newspaper starting in 1995 and continuing to the present. He has typed out over 300 articles, stories avidly read by fliers, visitors, out-of-towners and local folk. And he occasionally drops down to the USFS hangar to swap yarns with the current crop of government pilots, passing along some of the sage knowledge he gained during his years on floats.

Among old and bold pilots, Chick Beel is a living legend.

Bush pilot Chick Beel

NOSE FIRST *in the* WOODS BY BOB CARY

*H*e was a chipper 95 years old when we interviewed him. Milt Nelson began flying March 16, 1934, he recalled exactly. "I was living in Superior, Wisconsin, at that time, and my friend Russ Ericson called to say he had a deal to buy a used airplane and would I care to learn how to fly? Sounded like a great idea so when Russ bought that open-cockpit Travelair, we proceeded to take lessons and my career in the air began."

They accumulated about 500 hours of air time, much of it flying out of the Grand Lakes air strip, which Milt noted was not more than an extended vegetable garden. He recalled landing on skis at Gull Lake one winter night when they were heading for Tuscarora Lake on a fishing expedition. "Night caught us and we landed, taxied to shore, built a fire and sat up all night feeding wood into the fire at fifty below."

This was before there was adequate antifreeze, thus they had drained the water and oil out of the plane for the night. In the morning, they heated the oil and water and put it back in the plane. There were no electric starters on most small planes then, and engines were started by turning the prop over by hand. Although Milt's fishing buddy was a beefy 200 pounds, he couldn't turn over the prop. "He was chinning himself on the blade and still it wouldn't budge," he laughed.

To get the prop loose, Milt pulled a blow torch out of his tool kit and aimed the flame at the hub. Eventually, the combination of the hot oil, hot water and blowtorch allowed the prop to be spun, and the engine started so they could continue their fishing trip. "Caught some trout, too," Milt recalled.

Nelson became a pilot for the U.S. Forest Service on the Superior National Forest in 1942. He retired after 20 years of flying the bush on floats and skis, some of it under fairly harrowing conditions.

Milt Nelson (l) with District Ranger Bill Trygg

Among his memoirs was a trip flying a timber survey for the Forest Service in a Stinson on floats. "The plane had two seats, side by side, so the extra man sat on some Duluth packs behind us. He had a seat belt but sat on the packs."

Near Dumbell Lake, the engine quit. Milt flipped the key to the reserve tank although he thought he should have had plenty of gas. The engine caught briefly, then sputtered and went silent. "We were coming down and nothing to do but fly her in," Milt remembered.

They crashed into the trees, shearing off tree tops, then trunks and finally plowing into the ground. "Hitting all the trees slowed us down a little," said Milt. "But when the floats hit the dirt, they dug in and we flipped over upside down. The seat belt snapped holding the guy sitting on the packsacks and he came flying forward, went between the timber cruiser and myself and wound up with his face at my feet against the rudder pedals."

The wings, fuselage and floats were crumpled up, but oddly enough, nobody got more than a scratch. "They took some photos of that bunched up wreck," Milt laughed. "You could never figure how anybody got out of it alive."

Of course, the Forest Service hierarchy was in a high state of agitation and Milt was suspended pending an investigation. The agency blamed him for the wreck, insisting he had failed to check his gas supply even though there was the smell of gas all around the wreck.

Investigators arrived, went over the wreck in detail and finally traced the problem to a magneto wire that had become frayed and shorted out in flight. However, the agency never admitted the accident was caused by faulty maintenance. Milt had done nothing wrong except perhaps take off in a plane waiting to have a wreck. In any event, he was reinstated and finished up his 20 years of flying for the government.

After that, he flew for Al West, Ernie "Hoot" Hautala and some of the other operators using Ely as a base.

USFS Stinson wrinkled up in the woods

"One thing we were always concerned with when flying canoes, was making sure we had the canoes tied snug to the floats," Milt said. "One time Oscar Ringnell was supposed to fly a canoe somewhere, but he was having a difficult time getting it lashed on the floats."

Ringnell had a reputation for nipping the bottle, and while he was wobbling around the dock at Ely trying to tie a canoe on the plane, he slipped and fell between the pontoon and the dock. This should have been a pretty good indication that he was probably in poor condition to fly, but he was unfazed, eventually got the ropes snugged down, climbed in the plane and took off for Lac La Croix. He had no further mishaps and came in with a smooth landing at La Croix. The only problem was, all he had on the left pontoon were the ropes. The canoe was missing. He flew back with resort owner Martin Skala, looking for the missing watercraft, which was spotted by Martin hanging nose-down in a tree. "Martin said the canoe never hit the ground," Milt recalled. "It must have just sailed down and when it went into the woods, went in bow-first, caught in a treetop and stuck there. Didn't hurt the canoe a bit."

The amazing part of the incident was that the canoe came off the pontoon and missed the entire tail section of the plane. In other cases where canoes had broken loose, they took off the rudder or elevator, causing an immediate crash.

"Ringnell led a charmed life," Milt said. "Even when drinking, he got away with a whole lot more than any sober pilot would have."

When Milt was flying for the government, so was the legendary Chick Beel, another pilot who had some instruction under the G.I. Bill. "One morning we had seven government V.I.P.s to fly on an inspection of the Boundary Waters," Milt noted. "Normally Chick would have drawn the assignment. However, he called in saying he was awfully sick and for me to take the group. I met them at the seaplane base, and as we were getting set to go, I was astonished to hear Chick singing his best rendition of 'Come to Me My Melancholy Baby' from the office off the main hangar. Chick had a pretty good voice and liked to sing when he worked. So here was that unmistakable voice echoing through the hangar when Chick was supposed to be home sick."

Milt took a sip of coffee and continued: "I went into the office where Chick was working and asked him just what the heck he was doing when he was too sick to fly. Chick said, 'When I don't feel good, I sing. And the louder I sing, the better I feel.' And went right on with 'Melancholy Baby' at the top of his lungs."

Milt followed quickly with another tale. "When Galen Pike was the supervisor of the Superior National Forest, he was a very much respected and oft-quoted official. He loved the wilderness very much and when he died, his final wish was to have his ashes sprinkled on Lac La Croix in the wilderness."

The new Supervisor, John Wehrnam, was presented with Galen's ashes in a brass urn by the widow.

"It was my job," noted Milt, "to fly John and the urn over La Croix so we could dispose of Galen's remains. We made it up to La Croix in the Beaver, circled the lake and John stuck his hand out the window with the urn. Unfortunately, the lid flew off and the whole load of ashes blew back into the cockpit, all over the walls, the seats, our clothes, in our eyes, and in our hair. We were even spitting Galen out of our teeth. I guess some of his ashes made it down to the lake, at least the urn did. We flew back to Ely, cleaned up the plane and ourselves, and we never told anyone about it until after the widow died."

Milt Nelson (r) with angler

FLYING INTO *the* FIRE

BY BOB CARY

*W*hen bush pilots get too old to fly, they still talk flying and like to hang out around floatplane operations. Two U.S. Forest Service veterans, Walt Newman at 84 and Milt Nelson, 95, make bi-monthly pilgrimages to the seaplane hangar on Shagawa Lake to watch maintenance work in progress and to talk shop with the current pilots. Almost every day they meet for morning coffee and flying talk at one of Ely's local eateries, an activity they were kind enough to share with me upon occasion.

We hardly had the sugar stirred into our coffee when Walt observed, "The greatest boost to flying in the United States was World War II."

Not just the war itself, he noted, which resulted in thousands of new pilots, but what was known as the G.I. Bill, a federal program for veterans providing advanced free education. Under the G.I. Bill, former service personnel could attend college, even take flying lessons at a qualified airfield near home. Airports all over the nation were busy with would-be fliers.

"There were 42 student pilots in Ely alone under the G.I. Bill," Walt explained. "A lot of them went into floatplane flying, learning under experienced fliers like Bill Leithold who operated one of the very early floatplane services in Northern Minnesota."

Walt picked up his rating under the G.I. Bill and continued on to commercial work. A whole new stable of pilots became available for floatplane operations at a time when bush flying was hitting a peak. Newman flew with the Forest Service from 1957 to 1977, taking the mandatory 20-year retirement.

Both of these old time bush pilots also flew some extracurricular work for commercial operators during Ely's heyday as the floatplane capital of North America.

Walt was born in Deer River, Minnesota, and became interested in aircraft while a member of the U.S. Air Force in World War II. However, he was not involved with flying. He was assigned to maintenance and worked on aircraft engines, a skill that came in handy after his discharge from service. He began flying under the G.I. Bill for veterans in a flying school conducted by Bill Leithold at his seaplane base on Sandy Point in Ely.

"There were forty of us," Walt recalled. "We flew a J-3 Cub, an Aeronca Champ and a Stinson. Two of us, Chick Beel and I, went on to fly commercially for Leithold, starting at his base in Ely where I also did engine maintenance. When Leithold moved to Green Bay, Wisconsin, I went down there for three years, from 1954 to 1956. Most of the flying was on wheel planes, but Bill had a few planes on floats at De Pere on the Fox River, including a twin-engine Cessna 210, a Fairchild and a Cessna 190. We used those to fly people to Canada by way of Sault St. Marie."

While employed at Green Bay, Walt studied and earned credentials in Inspection Authorization and was later involved with dozens of annual aircraft inspections under the FAA.

"I did a lot of maintenance at the Green Bay Airport and then applied and got on with the U.S. Forest Service at Ely, mostly on maintenance, but also some flying. As time went on, I was involved with more and more flying, less and less maintenance until I did nothing but fly."

He worked closely with Chick Beel and with the other personnel at the Ely base when Chick began to experiment with the snorkel system that was being developed for picking up water with a moving aircraft, the forest fire control system now used extensively all across North America. After his retirement, Walt flew for Pat Magie, but the era of Ely floatplanes was over.

Walt Newman cradled his coffee cup with both hands and stared out the front window of the café, taking note of the deep blue June sky with patches of white fleece moving west to east at a leisurely pace. His eyes twinkled as he assessed the day and allowed that it would be about as smooth up in the sky as a pilot could experience.

"There is something about flying on a nice, clear day when you can see an endless panorama of green forest and blue lakes, stretching clear to the horizon. You feel like you are a king and everything spread out below is yours…it all belongs to you."

"Yeah," added his coffee pal, Milt Nelson. "Up there it is like an eagle, circling over the whole world stretched out below."

"The only trouble with a bright, sunshiny day without wind," noted Walt, "was that the ride sometimes got too smooth and a pilot was likely to doze off."

"You ever go to sleep in the air?" asked Milt.

"Oh, boy!" Walt laughed out loud, then took another sip of his coffee. "Take a warm, quiet day when you're flying alone, nobody to talk to, and with the sun shining on the windshield...it's easy to fall asleep. I don't think I ever slept for more than five minutes or so, but I knew when I woke up that I had been asleep. The first thing, I started looking around, trying to figure out where I was...which lakes I was flying over."

"Ever have any little tricks to keep awake?" Milt asked.

"Yeah. Fly with the windows open to let the cool air come in."

"Ever land to try and get the sleep out of your system?" Milt inquired.

"Oh, yeah. Sometimes I landed and went swimming. Dove right off the floats. The cold water would wake me up pretty quick.

"Of course, there were other days and every day was different." Milt nodded in agreement. "I can remember a lot of times we weren't flying in sunshine and clear skies. There were the days we had howling winds...days I didn't really care for. Those were always the worst days for fire and on some of those days I would just as soon not be flying. Whenever we had a fire and had to water-bomb under gusty conditions, that was always a challenge."

Walt looked out toward the street. His eyes narrowed as he re-lived some big fires he had flown in. "Flying in crown fire conditions was a real hazard. Sometimes, there was only one of us on the scene to start with...one plane to keep fire bombing a blaze until a crew could be brought in. That single plane, wetting down the woods a load at a time, was often all that kept the forest from having a major fire. Unless you've been up there you can have no idea how fast a fire can move in a strong wind."

He recalled the Little Indian Sioux Fire, named for the river flowing into the wilderness between Crane Lake and Ely. This was a "controlled" early spring burn that went out of control in sudden high winds. "We flew out of Jeanette Lake...that's where we picked up our water," Walt shook his head. "That was some fire! When it crowned out there was simply no stopping it. We just tried to contain it and keep it from getting worse."

Walt Newman and Milt Nelson on U.S. Forest Service dock

The fire, which consumed thousands of acres of forest, was roaring toward Ontario's Quetico Provincial Park and the Canadian city of Atikokan, when the wind suddenly switched 180 degrees, from southwest to northeast, blowing the fire back on itself. In addition, snow began falling. Within 24 hours, what had all the elements of a major disaster was brought under control by weary crews on the ground and in the air.

"I remember the Nina-Moose Fire," Walt said suddenly. "An island was on fire and I called it in, then started water-bombing the island, wetting down everything. I knew that if the fire really got going it would jump from the island to the shore and we would have a real project on our hands.

"Waino Wirtanen arrived on the ground to organize a crew and I kept hauling one load of water after another. It was tight getting the plane in and out of there with smoke and everything, especially getting out with loads of water. Waino said every time I went out, I was knocking branches off the trees. But we held it from getting away and finally got it out," he added.

"Other times it was just routine flying," Walt observed. "Not much going on. We used to say we had hours and hours of boredom punctuated by minutes of sheer terror."

U.S. Forest Service Beaver dropping a load of water

For a few moments they reminisced about the time the engine in Milt's plane quit and he went into the trees by Dumbell Lake. "When the engine quits," Milt noted, "you don't try anything fancy…you just fly it down into the woods and hope for the best."

"Nobody ever had much practice flying an aircraft into the woods," Walt laughed. "If it happened and you survived, you hoped it only happened once."

He brought up the matter of luck, something all pilots believe in. "Milt and I are both around because of luck," Walt paused and thought a moment. "Of course, some of that luck was because we paid attention to details, like fuel. We always checked our fuel and made sure we had enough for the trip. You can't believe how many pilots got into trouble because they guessed they had enough gas, but didn't check."

"Another scary thing for some pilots was flying on instruments in rain, snow or fog. It's like flying in nothing. No up, down or sideways."

"I was never very good with instruments," Milt confessed. "Did you do much with instruments?"

"Yeah," Walt took a big pull on his coffee. "Out of some 40 or so pilots who trained on the G.I. Bill after World War II, three of us got our commercial licenses and took a lot of instrument work. We all got our rating and I think every pilot should be checked out on instruments. When you get into a situation where you're flying

34

blind, it is no time to start wishing you knew how to use instruments."

Funny thing," Walt added as he drained his coffee cup, "the closest I ever came to smashing up a plane wasn't in the air. It was on the water."

He thought back for a moment. "Bill Leithold had me fly Paul Summer's wife to their resort at the top of Pipestone Falls at the entrance to Basswood Lake. I was flying the Aeronca Champ," he noted. "I dropped Mrs. Summer off at their dock. I had the ignition and the throttle set so all I had to do was turn over the engine and it would start up. So I pushed the floats away from the dock and kicked over the prop. Only it wouldn't start. I tried several times and figured some dirt or something had gotten into the system. There was nothing to do but paddle back to the dock and fix the problem, so I climbed down on the float to reach the paddle we kept lashed up under the fuselage. Only it wasn't there! Somebody had used it and didn't put it back.

"In the meantime, I realized the Champ and I were drifting with the current toward the falls. I could picture going down the falls in the plane, having it demolished on the rocks. I yelled at Mrs. Summer to jump in a canoe and hurry out with a paddle. While she set about doing this, I tried frantically to get the engine going again.

"Just before she got to me, the engine suddenly caught and I was able to taxi away from the falls and take off. Every now and then I think of what a mess the falls would have made out of the Champ and me, too, if we had gone into it."

He recalled some of the very early pilots, like Hoot Hautala. "Hoot was not only a good pilot, he was a great mechanic," Walt related. "Well, maybe ingenious is a better word than great. He had the ability to figure out ways to repair and even modify airplanes that were possibly not orthodox but seemed to function. Once he was working on a means of changing the pitch of a propeller to get more lift on takeoff and some of us were watching him at the seaplane base."

Walt thought back and continued: "Somebody said to Hoot that if there was a way to get more thrust out of a propeller, the airplane manufacturers would have done it."

"'What does the factory know?' Hoot said. 'They just make 'em, they don't fly 'em.'"

Walt recalled when they had to fly emergencies for lost canoe campers, injured canoe campers, sick canoe campers and sometimes dead canoe campers. They also had some odd cases that were more or less emergencies. "Once we had someone call up who said this guy's wife was terribly ill and would we try to contact her husband who was on a canoe trip so he could return home immediately. We called around to find out who outfitted the trip and where he might be, and finally sort of pinpointed Thomas Lake where we might find his camp. After some searching and a few stops at different campsites, we taxied up to the right campsite and found the husband chopping fire wood. We told him that we had received a phone call that his wife was desperately ill and wanted him to come home.

"'Frankly, I don't give a darn if she dies,' he said, and went right on chopping wood."

Milt had heard that same story many times before, but he laughed just as loud as he had the first time. The clock on the restaurant wall was moving on. Walt and Milt finished up their coffee and walked slowly out of the café, climbed into Milt's car and headed for home.

STAYING IN THE AIR

"After school, on weekends and all summer long, kids, especially boys, would throng the waterfront, watching planes take off and land."

FLOATPLANES *and* FLOATING KIDS

BY BOB CARY

*W*hen the Ely seaplane operation stretched from Crossman Point, on the west side of Schaeffer Bay around past the Forest Service seaplane base, past all the commercial floatplane docks by Sarkipato's Resort all the way to Sandy Point, a distance of two miles, it was a mecca for kids. Given the excitement of planes on floats roaring in and out daily, over town, over Chandler mining location or Finn Hill, plus the adjacent lakeshore, it was inevitable that all the kids living anywhere near would congregate along the waterfront.

Even those kids who lived several blocks away from the lake could not escape the thrill of seeing float-equipped Curtiss Robins, Cessnas, Cubs, Aeroncas, Beeches, Fairchilds, DeHavilands, about anything that would fly, going over the tree-tops to land on Shagawa Lake. After school, on weekends and all summer long, kids, especially boys, would throng the waterfront watching planes take off and land. And wishing they, too, could be bush pilots. Some of them, like Chick Beel, who grew up near Sandy Point, Jack and Wiley Hautala, Joe Buckner, Bill Rom, and a host of others went on to take flying lessons as soon as they were old enough and had the cash.

The Shagawa Lake waterfront was like a magnet to kids, although a lot of parents didn't want their offspring hanging around the floatplane docks because of the danger from whirling props plus the water itself. Like most cities of the late 1800s and early 1900s, the municipal sanitary system consisted of a series of underground pipes that carried all the sewage downhill. That is, all that wasn't confined to backyard outhouses. In Ely's case, the sewage went downhill into Shagawa Lake. Included was the effluent from the Shipman Hospital, the schools, downtown shopping

40

area and most of the residential area. Unfortunately, all of this eventually drained from Shagawa into Fall Lake and thence into the federal Boundary Waters Canoe Area Wilderness, a not particularly healthy situation, especially for canoe campers who were using lake water for cooking. It was not until after World War II that the U.S. government set up an experimental program with a tertiary treatment plant at Ely to not only treat the human waste, but also to see if it was feasible to remove the phosphorus added by detergents.

Fortunately for Ely, there is a current in the lake, flowing from west to east, carried by the entry of relatively clean Burntside River and Armstrong Creek. The highly-enriched waters tended to flow toward the east, out of Shagawa Lake by way of the Shagawa River; but enough of the nutrient settled to the bottom and remained to richly fertilize the water, causing a spectacular, bright green algae bloom every summer. The lake looked like it was coated with a thick layer of bright green paint. This didn't have much effect on the planes going in and out but it may have had an effect on the kids who swam in it. And swim they did.

Moony Gotchnik, granddaughter of legendary French-Russian guide Andy Toutloff, was one of the kids who spent as much time in the water as on land. One of the more adventurous forms of recreation was to dive and swim around the floatplanes docked in the bay.

"The bush pilots didn't much like us swimming around their planes, and they used to yell at us to get away, but we swam there anyway," she recalls. One of their favorite sports was to watch for a plane loading up to take off, dive under and come up beneath the plane, between the floats and out of sight. When the pilot would turn over the engine and prepare to taxi away from the dock, the kids would reach up, grab the metal spreader bar holding the floats apart and hang on for a ride.

"We would go sailing across the bay as the plane picked up speed," Moony recalls. "But we had sense enough to always let go before the plane took off."

When caught, of course, the kid's parents were duly notified and the miscreant was usually subjected to discipline. That was in an era when it was not only customary for parents to exact corporal punishment, but was considered the only politically correct form of justice. Kids often got it twice: once for taking a ride under a moving floatplane and also for swimming in the polluted lake. But it didn't seem to have much of an overall effect other than make the kids more cautious.

Just up the shore, at Sarkipato's dock and boathouse, a bunch of kids, often the same ones, could be found on hot summer days diving out of the back of the boathouse, an activity that resulted in the police being notified on a regular basis.

Marie Sarkipato Erickson, one of the ringleaders, explains it this way: "It wasn't so much the diving and swimming, but the fact that we usually went skinny dipping because many of us didn't own swimming suits. That co-ed skinny dipping aroused the anger of the neighbors who thought such activity was downright sinful. We had one neighbor lady who would keep a sharp eye on the Sarkipato boathouse, and if she spied some bare bodies glistening in the sun, would immediately call the police station.

"It was not particularly easy for the police to make an arrest because the boathouse was connected to the shore by a long plank runway. Usually, we could spot the policeman on his way, which gave us time to get our clothes on or jump in the lake and escape behind dock piers.

"My brother began complaining to my mother that she should purchase a swimming suit for me when I as about nine years old, saying that it was not right for me to be swimming nude with the boys. So my mother bought me a swimming suit. In the meantime, however, my brother got an idea on how to discourage police surveillance. One hot summer day, when we all decided to go for a swim, my brother got a pail of axle grease and a paint brush. He started at the shore and painted a layer of grease on the plank all the way out to the boathouse. Then we went swimming. Sure enough, our nosy neighbor called the cops, and we didn't know about it until we heard a loud yell and a great splash as the cop came charging down the plank to make the arrest, hit the grease and went flying off into the lake.

"I think we all got a whipping for that one, but we thought it was worth it."

Swimming in polluted Shagawa Lake, in and around the seaplane docks, may not have been the healthiest activity kids could have engaged in, but some of the old-timers point out that a lot of those kids grew up and survived to a ripe old age. Some say that anybody who swam in Shagawa Lake in those days and didn't die young probably developed an immunity to everything that could possibly afflict the human race.

Ely's seaplane base in the 1940s

FLYIN' AROUND

*W*iley Gregg was a flier who seemed totally lacking in fear. He tried a lot of things in some wild weather that many pilots would not dream of tackling. However, this incident occurred in good, but cold, weather; it was just a little different. It had to do with a winter pageant at Pike Lake near Duluth. Like most who flew, Wiley could always use a little extra cash. He had rented Pat Magie's Cessna 180 on skis and was taking passengers up for rides over Duluth at ten bucks a head.

Things were going well until one takeoff when he had a hard time getting the tail up and the plane into flying attitude, even with plenty of speed. Normally, during a takeoff run with a tail-wheel type airplane, the tail will raise with a little forward pressure on the control wheel. But on this takeoff, Wiley was surprised that every time he tried to lift the tail, it immediately went back down to the snow. As his ground speed finally went over 50 miles an hour, the tail came up and the airplane sprang into the air. He puzzled about this until he landed and dropped off his passengers when he found out what caused the plane's strange behavior.

In the winter, most planes flew with about 16 feet of rope trailing from the tail wheel. The rope was used to turn the planes around on the ice. Wiley's wife was the ticket seller for the event and she noticed that when Wiley was taxiing to take off, seven kids ran out of the crowd, grabbed the rope to see how long they could hang on, slipping and sliding as the plane accelerated over the frozen surface. At 50 miles per hour they all fell off the rope, flying every whichway. The tail came up and Wiley was airborne. Outside of a lot of snow down their collars and in their boots, none of the kids suffered any ill effects. But Wiley made sure nobody was hanging on the rope from that point on.

BACK WHEN IT ALL STARTED

BY JACK HAUTALA

*M*y dad, Ernie Hautala, also known as "Hoot," started his flying days in Tower, Minnesota, in the 1930s. There was no airport in Tower so they used Lake Vermilion in the summer, at least the fliers who had floats on their airplanes. In the winter, when the lake was frozen, they used skis. Spring and fall, when the lake was in transition, thawing or freezing, they needed a landing field where they could keep the planes, one close as possible to Lake Vermilion.

Wally Holm and Hoot Hautala (r)

About the only spot suitable was Branwall's field, a small strip of grassy meadow surrounded by high weeds and brush, hardly big enough for a plane to squeeze in or out. Fortunately, those old crates used in the 1930s had slow landing speeds and a pilot could cut power and nearly stall them into a landing.

One trick my dad used to slow down his landing was to wrap wire tightly around the tail wheel so it wouldn't turn. When the plane hit the ground, that immobile wheel acted like a brake and allowed for better control on tail wheel-type aircraft.

Hoot Hautala, flying in all seasons

One of the early planes Dad flew was an open cockpit Waco, common at that time. On one landing, even with all his skill, Dad overran Branwall's field and rolled through the fence at the end. Not much damage was done to the plane but the fence needed repairs.

Talk about raw courage! Some of these guys even flew out of Branwall's field at night, quite an operation when one considers the field had no lights and had to be picked out of the darkness by the location of nearby house lights plus the pilot's memory of how the land lay in daylight. Dad would come in, throttle back, lean out of the open cockpit and listen to brush hitting the wheels. When he didn't hear any more rustling, he knew he was over the grassy field, cut the power entirely and dropped in.

One might ask why anyone would be flying at night. Well, nobody in the Depression had any money, particularly those who flew. They were always broke, always looking for ways to save money or make a little cash for airplane gas, tires, repairs and whatever. Like a lot of our neighbors, our family ate a lot of moose and deer meat obtained in the forest, sometimes not in hunting season. Dad always had a carcass or two cached on a lakeshore, a hidden meat supply within easy reach by the plane.

Hoot Hautala

Unidentified woman, Hoot and Dorothy Molter

Making money during the Depression required a lot of ingenuity and entrepreneurial spirit, perhaps even a little fudging with the law. Back in the 1930s, one lucrative but risky enterprise involved flying trappers into Canadian lakes, preferably in Quetico Park where trapping was prohibited, and flying the beaver and otter fur out a week or two later.

Pilots who were engaged in this type of operation knew that game wardens and customs officers would be on the lookout for planes coming to Ely, so my dad would fly the furs down to a small lake near Uncle Axel's farm. He would unload them there and fly back to land at Ely with the plane nice and clean with no contraband on board. Later he would drive to Axel's farm in the car, pick up the furs and take them to a fur buyer who would wink at their origin.

Somehow, the agents got wind of this and once raided the farm, but could not find the furs, which were well concealed. However, they spotted Dad and asked Axel who that was. Uncle Axel said he was just a hired hand, and Dad was very busy tossing cow manure with a fork. They never made the connection that he was a pilot.

Hoot gassing up his plane

MOB DAYS

BY JACK HAUTALA

When the Chicago and Minneapolis gangsters were in their heyday, just before and right after World War II, some of them hung out in the north country when on vacation or on the lam. We had a number of them around Ely, some who came up to go fishing and usually to bring along their artillery for pistol practice on tin cans floating in the lakes. One group of these Chicago citizens bought a cabin on Horse Lake, which became a popular vacation spot where they could relax in a remote area from the stress of their business without having to worry about rival gang members sneaking in to assassinate them. Tony Cohen was a leader of this group and my dad flew him with his wife and his friends to their cabin on a number of trips. I was a youngster at that time and acted as a busboy, carrying their luggage from the parking lot to the floatplane. They were genial and heavy tippers.

Tony was a very friendly and generous guy and one time gave my dad an expensive leather jacket right off his back. We knew about the target shooting because once Harry Anderson flew some supplies to Horse Lake and said the whole waterfront was covered with splashes where pistol bullets were churning up the water.

One day, two new guys we had never seen before came to town and paid Dad to fly them up to Tony's camp on Horse Lake. The next day word filtered down that Tony had been shot in an accident. My dad immediately flew up to see what was going on. The two young guys met him at the dock and insisted on being flown out right now. When Dad got them to town, they hopped in their car and left, which made my mother suspicious because she thought they should at least stick around for the sheriff. Turned out Tony had been shot in the back of the head and the story was that the gang was shooting at turtles and somehow Tony had the

49

bad luck to walk into the line of fire. The sheriff questioned everyone at the camp but could not get a whole lot of information. The two strangers had left before the sheriff arrived and never were questioned.

Tony had a very good looking redheaded wife named Ginger and we thought it somewhat strange that she later came back to Horse Lake with the guy who was supposed to have shot Tony. Later we heard they both had bad luck and were shot to death in Chicago. Tony Cohen had one last piece of good luck. He is enjoying the peace and solitude of the Ely cemetery.

TRADE *on the* SIDE

BY JACK HAUTALA

*T*here are all kinds of stories about pilots sneaking over into Canada to pick up a load of contraband whiskey before prohibition was repealed in 1934. Later, when booze was legal, they would fly in a load of Canadian rye without paying the U.S. Customs duty and this was not necessarily confined to the Depression era.

Kenny Christian, the veteran U.S. Customs Officer at Ely, often complained that political big shots from St. Paul and Washington, D.C., sometimes flew in from fishing trips in Canada, landed at the Ely mayor's dock on Burntside Lake, unloaded their whiskey and then called Kenny to come and inspect the empty plane. This irritated Kenny a lot because all incoming planes were supposed to fly into the public seaplane dock to be checked. He reported a number of violations to his superiors in St. Paul but was told to just check out the planes as they reported in and not get too inquisitive about the big shots.

Fish were a source of revenue, too, and a few pilots would fill their floats partially full with walleyes or lake trout and fly back to the U.S. to make the sale. This required a Canadian accessory who would net fish for a piece of the action. Canadians were just as eager to make money as any Yank. It was sort of an international trade arrangement.

LATTER DAY PIRATES

BY BOB CARY

One of the extracurricular fish operators I knew quite well was Merle Thoms. I knew Merle because he played accordion in the same dance band where I played drums. Merle was operating during the 1980s, usually flying fishermen into Ontario and flying them out with a couple limits of fish. After flying to a lake in Canada, he guided the fishermen by canoe or boat and took the fish out by air, because he could sneak more fish out that way. Merle was just trying to make a living, but the Canadians take a dim view of Americans earning money on Canadian soil, particularly without proper papers. Merle didn't have a resort operator's license or any of the other necessary permits, so he was always a suspect. He was also a guy who couldn't stand prosperity.

The Canadians didn't bother him a whole lot until he started getting bolder. He scouted some of the lakes up near Atikokan and found where Canadian resort operators kept their boats tied. Merle proceeded to take fishermen up to those lakes and would "borrow" a boat for a day without asking the owner. Merle had guts, but he had one fatal flaw: he liked to talk.

One day, coming out of a lake where he borrowed some Canadian's boat, he was hiking down the trail with two fishermen and a stringer full of walleyes. He ran into a couple other fishermen going into the same lake and proudly showed off his catch. And he presented the two fishermen with his business card and told them if they ever wanted to get walleyes like these, give him a call. The trouble was, the two strangers were Canadian law enforcement officers who were looking for Merle. They promptly put him under arrest, took his fish, fishing tackle and confiscated the van he used to transport anglers to the lakes and booked him for a court date with a long list of law violations. He managed to get out of Canada via the floatplane, but the Canadian police impounded his van to hold as security for the court appearance. Merle had no intention of appearing on all the charges in a Canadian court so he simply didn't show up. The last we knew, the van was still in the police yard at Thunder Bay, Ontario.

HIGH FLYING

BY BOB CARY

*O*ne unsavory airborne activity that began in the "flower children" era of the '60s and '70s involved flying drugs into the U.S. from Canada. Some of this was done by Canadian bush pilots who were pretty cute. They would fly a load of junk over a pre-arranged lake near the International Line and without landing, drop it into the water for dealers from the U.S. to pick up by boat. Mostly this was marijuana, bundled up in waterproof bags. What we knew about this enterprise was confirmed by fishermen who called to say they found a bag on this or that lake and turned it in. Perhaps the pilot, in the dark, dropped it in the wrong lake or maybe there was some other disconnect. No question but what Canadian and U.S. enforcement people were, and are, ever on the lookout for funny stuff crossing the line.

WOLF PATROL

BY BOB CARY

*U*p until the mid-60s, there was a $35 bounty on timber-wolves. The idea behind this was that by eliminating wolves, other species such as deer, would greatly increase. Wolf fur was also valuable, so that hunters taking wolves could realize from $40 to $50 total. One wolf could bring in more than two or three days' wages. It also provided extra cash for bush pilots who capitalized on their aerial mobility.

In the winter, with deep snow on the ground, it was not particularly difficult to locate wolf packs adjacent to lakes. A skilled pilot could herd the wolves out of the woods and onto the ice where they were vulnerable to shooting. Originally, the wolf patrol was made up of two-man teams, one flying and one shooting. The pilot would drop down at reduced speed, hit the snow-packed surface on his skis and taxi close to the running wolves. The shooter, armed with a shotgun and buckshot, would lean out the door of the speeding plane and pick off the running wolves as they came within range. All of this required excellent timing and also some careful flying. There were instances where the pilots became absorbed in the shooting and wound up flying the plane into the woods.

The two-man teams meant the wolf bounty had to be split two ways, a problem with pilots who were chronically broke. Elwyn West was one of the first to devise a means of one-person flying and shooting in order to collect the entire bounty. He would come down near a running pack, set the throttle, lock the stick between his knees and shoot out the window while steering the plane with his knees. Other pilots began doing the same thing with more or less success. One of these was Frank Baltich, Jr., who kept his plane at West's Seaplane Base on Shagawa Lake. Frank worked a shift in the iron mines and would hunt wolves in his spare time, usually with his younger brother Joe as gunner. But on one occasion when flying alone, Frank spotted a wolf pack on Jackfish Bay of Basswood Lake and determined to try West's system. He dropped his skis down on the snow, put the stick between his knees, opened the window and prepared to shoot. Unfortunately, his skis hit a snowdrift, the plane ground looped and his 65-horse J3 Piper Cub plowed in on its nose and splintered the wooden propeller. Normally, he carried a pair of snowshoes lashed to a wing strut, but on that particular day, he had to slog out in boots through deep drifts.

Ordering and getting a new prop from the Piper Company was time-consuming and Frank wanted to get his stranded plane out of the woods right away. He contacted a friend who owned an air-boat powered by a propeller with the same hub diameter although with a somewhat smaller blade size. West flew Frank to the damaged plane on Jackfish Bay where the smaller prop was bolted in place. Whatever was wrong with the down-sized prop, or perhaps damage to the engine when the plane nosed over, they never found out. When Frank took off for Ely, the engine exploded over Newton Lake.

His first move was to jerk open the door and make sure the aircraft was not on fire. Next, he nosed down and landed the crippled plane on Newton Lake. Once again he walked out of the woods.

Frank had now lost two days' work at his mine job in pursuit of wolves and knew if he missed another day he was apt to get fired. He enlisted the help of Elwyn West to fine a new engine and replace the blown-out power plant on Newton Lake. West found a new engine in Duluth, still in the crate. He trucked it to Ely and attempted to load it into another Cub with the help of Frank's younger brother Joe.

Joe Baltich recalls all the trouble they had trying to get the crated engine into West's craft to fly it out. "We finally had to remove it from the crate," Joe remembered. "Even without the crate, it hardly fit in the limited passenger space. Part of it hung outside and we were unable to get the right door shut."

West roped the engine to inside struts with clothesline and told young Joe to sit on the engine, hanging onto the rope. There was scant room for Joe and he rode holding onto the rope with his rear end hanging out in the wind, wondering what kind of a ride he and the engine would have to the ground if the rope broke.

El West made it to Newton Lake without mishap, landed and taxied over to Frank's disabled Piper. They shoveled the snow away down to bare ice, then unloaded the new engine onto the ice. They went to the nearby woods and cut three thick saplings, which they hauled out on the lake to use for a tripod. From this they suspended a hoist, lifted the broken engine out of the plane and bolted the new one in. It was bitter cold and they kindled a fire on shore. Every few minutes they ran to the fire so West could warm up his hands. Late in the evening, West was hurrying because his fingers were freezing.

"I don't think he got everything in there right," Joe commented. "But we finished up and left."

The next day it was snowing when West flew Joe and Grandpa Baltich back to Newton Lake with ten gallons of gas, some food in a packsack and instructions to start up the new engine and run it slow and fast for a break-in period.

"The new engine started right up," Joe recalled. "We set the throttle and went over to shore and built a fire. While we were sitting there, listening to the engine, I thought I heard some extra sounds and I told grandpa. He said he could hear nothing wrong."

At 4 p.m., El flew in with Frank to get the Cub out. Joe told them about the strange engine sounds. They listened but heard nothing. Joe and Grandpa flew back with Frank in West's plane and El West flew Frank's plane home with the new engine. When they landed at Rolando's Bay on Shagawa Lake and tied up, El said, "You're right, Joe. There is something wrong with that engine."

He pulled off the cowl and went to work on it, discovering he had hooked two wires in backward when he replaced the blown engine. "He was lucky to make it back," Joe noted.

"I never owned a plane, but I flew a lot with my brother Frank," he said. "When he got his first Piper Cub, I was in high school and I read the whole owner's manual, cover to cover. I had my first ride in the plane on a cold, damp day in 1946. We made a trip out over the canoe country, and on the way back, the engine began to sputter and miss. Frank had only about 40 hours in the air and didn't really know what to do.

"'I think you've got to put the carburetor heat about half on,' I said. 'It's probably forming ice.'

"Frank looked at me like I was nuts but he set the carburetor heat control at the halfway point. The engine noise cleared up and we flew back just fine. 'How did you know about that?' Frank asked. 'They never said anything about carburetor heat when I was taking flying lessons.'

"'I read the handbook,' I answered.

"'What book?' Frank asked.

"'It's called "How to Fly" and it came with your Piper Cub.'

"'Gimme the book back,' Frank said, 'I'm gonna read it.'"

There were hundreds of wolves shot around Ely, Grand Marais and International Falls before researchers determined that paying out bounties was simply a waste of the taxpayers' money. By the early 1960s, there was a bill in the State Legislature to abolish the bounty although it was still popular with trappers and hunters.

Former District Forest Ranger Bill Trygg was a State Representative at that time and he phoned constituents asking what to do. "They've got this bill up to abolish the wolf bounty," he pointed out. "What do you think?"

"The studies show it's a waste of money," some said.

"Yeah, I think so, too," Trygg observed. "But if I vote to eliminate the wolf bounty it will make a lot of people mad."

"Well, you've got to figure it out for yourself," he was told.

When the bill came up, Trygg voted to eliminate the wolf bounty. In the next election, the people of his district voted to eliminate Bill Trygg.

The wolf bounty is long gone. So is Bill Trygg. The pilots who flew and shot wolves are mostly long gone. In their place is the new International Wolf Center in Ely, a huge educational facility housing mammoth displays and featuring a pack of live wolves in a natural-looking setting where visitors can watch them and take photos through large glass windows.

Thousands of tourists crowd the Wolf Center each summer, spending thousands of dollars to see live wolves—far more dollars than the few hundred generated each winter for bounties paid on dead wolves.

RESCUES & BRAVE TALES

"Some of the things I learned from Magie and the other old pilots are the reason I'm still around today."

BUSTING POACHERS *from* OVERHEAD BY BOB CARY

*L*ong before Bob Hodge became a flying game warden for the Minnesota Department of Natural Resources, he had thousands of hours in the air as a flight instructor and as a U.S. Air Force pilot. While much of his air time was on wheels, nearly all of his conservation work was on floats in the summer, skis in the winter. His ability to spot fish and game violations from the air became legendary and his methods of outwitting poachers were innovative.

"Most people," Hodge explains, "do not realize how much can be observed from the air, especially with a powerful set of field glasses. On these clear water lakes, you can even count the fish on a stringer tied to a boat."

Back when snowmobiles were a legal means of transportation in the Boundary Waters Canoe Area, several of us were lake trout fishing early one January Saturday through the ice on Ima Lake, maybe 30 miles east of the public landing on Moose Lake. It was a crisp 25° below with the sun edging up over the eastern rim of the forest like a dip of peach ice cream as we pulled in and parked against the shelter of a steep granite bluff on the lake's north side. It was a spot with a sheer dropoff into 60-and 70-foot ice water, a place where we had taken many nice trout over past years.

Our preferred spot was a sunken reef out in the middle of the lake but there were already eight snowmobiles and eight fishermen with lines down out there. Our group included Julian and Ruth Jones, Harry Lambirth, my wife and a Polaris snowmobile dealer from Tower named Gunderson. Behind his snowmobile, Jones had towed a sled with a power auger stowed inside along with our fishing tackle. It took only a few minutes for us to get holes drilled and lines in.

Gunderson was studying the eight fishermen out on the reef. "How come we've each got two lines out," Gunderson asked, "and those other guys have at least four lines each?"

"Mainly because we stay within the law," answered Jones.

"Well, who's gonna come all the way out here in the wilderness to check fish lines?"

"You'd be surprised," Jones commented dryly.

The sun was well up and we had a couple of trout on the ice when we heard the drone of a small plane coming from the west. The fishermen out on the reef ran to their holes and began reeling up the extra lines. However, the plane didn't come our way. It continued to the north and eventually vanished. The fishermen on the reef relaxed and began putting all their lines back in the holes.

"Who do you suppose that was?" Gunderson asked aiming the thumb of his mitten to where the plane had disappeared.

"That's Hodge, the game warden," was Harry's reply.

"He didn't even fly over to check those guys with all the extra lines," Gunderson complained.

"He doesn't have to," Jones said. "He can count the lines from the airplane with his field glasses."

Gunderson was puzzled. "Well, he must have seen all those lines...why didn't he fly over?"

"Wait," said Jones. "Just wait."

As the drone of the Cessna 180 vanished, silence settled in, broken only by an occasional call of distant ravens or a yell as one or another of the anglers across from us hauled a trout up on the ice, flashing like burnished silver in the frosty sunlight.

Suddenly, with only the faint sound of air whistling through the struts, the Cessna came in directly over the trees, power off, and skidded to a stop unerringly in the middle of the lines and fishermen out on the reef. The eight violators scrambled frantically, trying to kick their extra lines down the holes, but too late. Hodge was out of the plane, grabbing fishermen and rods right and left. He nailed the whole bunch and it took about a half hour to check all the identities, collect all the tackle and write up all the violations. Then he cranked up the Cessna and taxied over on aluminum skis to our spot to check our licenses. The eight unlucky fishermen started up their snowmobiles and headed for the trail back.

"Looks like you did pretty well out on the reef," Jones laughed as Hodge climbed down from his plane.

"Yeah," Hodge was noncommittal. "Few too many lines. One guy with no license. Going to be an expensive fishing trip for that bunch...I've got their fish and their tackle in the plane."

Besides being a highly skilled floatplane pilot, Hodge had an uncanny knack for locating lost hunters in the wilderness. A couple of times, those of us who served as volunteers on the Search and Rescue Ready Team saw the game warden in operation. One snowy November morning, long before daylight, the Search and Rescue unit was having coffee in Vertin's Restaurant in Ely, poring over maps and getting assignments. A quartet of deer hunters, operating out of Timber Trail Lodge on Farm Lake, planned to come out of the woods at suppertime. Three came out to find one of their group missing.

They tried signaling with auto horns and even fired off a few shots from their rifles as darkness closed in, but received no reply shots nor any sign of their missing companion. The lodge owner immediately called the sheriff and the search team prepared to roll at first light.

The three unlost hunters met with us at the restaurant and filled in some details. First, the lost hunter was not experienced and had never been in that area of forest before. Second, they were not sure if he had a map and even if he knew how to use one if he had it.

Search and Rescue members were all familiar with the lodge location at Farm Lake, situated on the rim of the 2,000-square-mile federal Boundary Waters Canoe Area Wilderness. Since the hunters went into the woods east of the resort, when they quit hunting they had only to head west to run into either the county road or Farm Lake. But if the lost hunter headed east, as feared, he had hundreds of miles of roadless wilderness in which to wander about and could be in real trouble.

The consensus of the sheriff's deputies and Search and Rescue members was that the hunter was probably somewhere on the shore of Farm Lake or in the woods nearby, hopefully sitting by a fire, waiting for help to arrive. But Hodge had a different take. He ran his finger over the map to the Kawishiwi river at a point about five miles east. "He's probably somewhere around here," he noted.

"That's five miles straight away from the lodge," somebody noted. "Why would he go 180 degrees away from the direction back?"

"Because he's lost," Hodge answered.

"But he couldn't have gotten clear over there," added another incredulous voice.

"Yeah, he could." Hodge studied the map. "People who are lost can travel a long way when they're scared."

Bob Hodge

The search team broke up and headed for the woods. It was just breaking daylight when wilderness guide Andy Hill and I aimed a resort boat up the east shore of Farm Lake, running the motor at half speed, eyeing the shore for any sign of smoke or a human figure. Other units, in twos and threes were similarly engaged plus a large contingent was spread out across the woods in a skirmish line, making a sweep through the area where the hunter had originally vanished. The roar of a DNR floatplane reverberated off the shoreline as Hodge took off, heading for the Kawishiwi River.

It was a frost-free November day, overcast and hazy. There was yet no snow on the ground, so it was impossible for anyone to track the lost hunter. Still, it hadn't gotten cold enough overnight for the hunter to freeze and we were confident he'd be found. An hour went by with Hill and I still scanning the lake shore as the outboard purred steadily.

Then, from the east, the state floatplane appeared, coming in just over the trees, heading straight for the lodge.

"Probably couldn't find the guy," Andy commented as we continued along the shoreline.

Moments later, we heard the sound of the sheriff's siren, signal for the searchers to return. We swung the boat around, opened the throttle and cut a wake back to the resort dock. The deputies and volunteers were assembled around Hodge and the rescued hunter who was tired, disheveled and obviously relieved to be back in civilization.

Like Hodge thought, he had traveled straight east about five miles from the resort and the road, crossing ridges and creeks to come out at last on the shore of the Kawishiwi River. At that point he had enough presence of mind to stop, or was perhaps too tired to continue; but he built a fire, assembled a stack of wood for the night and sat wondering if help was on the way. At daybreak, he tore off some balsam boughs and when he heard the search plane, threw them on the fire, sending up a column of smoke. Within minutes, the game warden taxied up and helped the weary and thoroughly embarrassed hunter into the cab of the plane.

Inside at the lodge, over cups of steaming coffee, we held a postmortem, the main question being how the game warden knew the lost hunter would be traveling east, away from where he started.

"I don't know," Hodge said, "but most of the time people who get lost seem to go 180 degrees away from where they should be going. Once I tracked a lost hunter north of Winton who headed straight for Canada. When I caught up with him, he had traveled several miles and in his panic crossed two roads, without even realizing it."

A few years back, Hodge was called out to search for two cross country skiers attempting to travel 45 miles on the Kekekabic Trail through the wilderness from the Gunflint Trail to the Fernberg Road, near Ely. The skiers were both experienced racers and considered the jaunt no more than an ordinary ski marathon, which could be completed in around four hours or perhaps a little more. To make time, they traveled as light as possible with some high energy snacks, water, a sleeping bag and a small nylon shelter, matches, compass and maps. They planned to follow the trail, well-marked for summer hiking, and push across in one day.

But there were a couple of unanticipated problems. One was

that the Kek Trail is not groomed and contains a number of obstacles. It is a hiking trail, although skiers have traveled on it. Second, their maps were incomplete. They had charts up to Thomas Lake, about half way across, and maps beyond Thomas Lake, but had no map showing Thomas Lake itself, which is fairly large. Third, and most important, the weather changed radically. A wet blizzard blew in the first day, piling up snow and making travel extremely difficult. Still, they were both in good condition and determined to make it. Night came early in the swirling flakes and they sought shelter to wait for daybreak.

As dawn crept in, the storm showed no sign of abating. Still they continued on, taking turns breaking trail through the ever-deepening snowdrifts. Trouble really reared its head when they came to Thomas Lake where their maps had a significant gap. Wet, cold, shaking uncontrollably, they attempted to start a fire. Later, one of the skiers recalled how disoriented he became as hypothermia set in.

He said he had a paper bag in his left hand to use as a fire starter, matches in his right. Every time he struck a match, the paper bag vanished from his left hand. He kept at it until the matches were gone. Next they heard auto traffic somewhere on their left, stepped out on Thomas Lake and spied a pickup truck and an ice fisherman. Figuring they were now out of trouble they abandoned their skis and walked out on the ice only to witness the ice fisherman disappear. Vaguely recognizing that they were hallucinating, they backtracked to their last position on the Kekekabic Trail and began plodding west toward the Fernberg Road.

At about the same time, their wives had become worried and had contacted the Lake County Sheriff. Bob Hodge was immediately notified but the howling blizzard prevented a takeoff. However, sheriff's deputy Martin Carlson, an old woods-wise hunter and trapper, strapped on his snowshoes and started from the west end of the Kek Trail, heading eastward to see if he could come across the missing skiers. Martin probably came within a mile of the skiers before darkness drove him back to the highway.

That night, the storm blew itself out and morning dawned clear and cold. Hodge was in the air immediately with the state plane, following the Kekekabic Trail eastward. He saw no smoke, no tracks, no sign of anyone. Dropping down to treetop level, he circled back and on nearby Disappointment Lake spotted a set of tracks and dropped down. As the skis on the Cessna cut through the drifts, he made out the form of a man leaning against a shoreline tree. Cutting the power, Hodge slipped out of the plane and walked toward the individual who seemed alert and all right, but surprised to see the airplane come in.

"We've been looking for you," Hodge said.

"Why is that?" the skier inquired.

"Your wives phoned the sheriff. They were worried."

"That's strange," the man exclaimed with a puzzled look. "I talked to my wife last night on the phone."

Hodge looked closer at the man. "What phone?"

"Back there," the man motioned vaguely toward the woods. "It was in a phone booth."

The game warden realized quickly that this individual was seriously disoriented. There are no phones in the wilderness.

"Where's your companion?" Hodge asked.

"He's OK," the man said. "He's sitting over by those trees."

Bob Hodge

Hodge spotted a snow-draped figure of a man slumped on the lake shore and walked over. Instantly he knew the man was dead and had been for some time. He also knew he had to get the survivor to medical help quickly or he might have a second casualty. With some persuasion, he got the man into the airplane, revved the engine and took off for Ely where an emergency crew met the plane at Shagawa Lake. Rushed to the hospital, the skier recovered completely and, surprisingly, had almost total recall of his ordeal, which he related to reporters as a means of warning others who might be tempted to make the same trek.

One of Hodge's hairiest flying adventures happened before his time with floatplanes, but is worth telling, nonetheless. As a transport pilot in the U.S. Air Force during World War II, he was assigned duty in the South Pacific flying cargo and personnel from island to island in a twin-engine C-47. During General Douglas MacArthur's retaking of the Philippines, Hodge was called upon to fly a USO entertainment troop to the island of Biak, recently captured by the U.S. Army. Thus he found himself over the ocean on a warm night with a planeload of musicians, singers and comedians heading for Biak, a piece of Pacific real estate he had visited before. As he flew on course toward the island he was surprised to hear the Biak controller break radio silence, something not usually done in a combat zone.

"You are to let down to 2,000 feet and hold that altitude. As you approach, we will advise you when to turn."

"What for?" Hodge asked.

"Never mind. Just hold at 2,000 feet and when you hear the command, give it hard left rudder. Over and out."

"Out," Hodge answered, pondering the strange radio communication.

A short time later he was looking out his starboard window and was startled to see the flame of an airplane exhaust from a ship right on his wing tip. Squinting into the darkness he made out the shape of a Japanese fighter-bomber traveling in close formation and suddenly realized what was going on. Because the U.S. anti-aircraft batteries were becoming extremely accurate and were downing a lot of Japanese planes, the enemy had taken to linking up with U.S. cargo planes flying into U.S. airfields where the Japanese would shoot down the cargo plane, then strafe and bomb the airfield.

Unwilling to break radio silence, Hodge flew grimly along, warily watching that telltale exhaust flare and wondering what lay ahead. As he came into Biak at 2,000 feet, the runway lights flashed on. At that exact moment, a voice crackled on the radio "Now!" the voice ordered.

Hodge lay the C-47 on its side, poured on the gas and cut a

90-degree bank to the left. At that moment, searchlights centered on the Japanese bomber, which was immediately engulfed in a deadly barrage of anti-aircraft fire, laid in at an exact range of 2,000 feet. The enemy plane blew up and crashed while Hodge landed his plane safely, and the USO show went on as planned.

THE TRIAL *of* GARY MITCHELL

BY BOB CARY

"*P*at Magie was not only an excellent pilot, he was an incredible teacher." Gary Mitchell set his cup of hot tea on the café table and grinned. "Some of the things I learned from Magie and the other old pilots are the reason I'm still around today."

Mitchell retired from flying in February 1999, after several decades of earning a living in the air. Some of his most memorable experiences occurred between 1971 and 1976 when he flew float-planes in the U.S.–Canadian bush out of Ely.

"There was the hot summer day in 1975 when I made two flights with the Twin Beech into Fourtown Lake," he recalled.

Fourtown Lake today is entirely within the federal wilderness, but in 1975 the wilderness line cut across the south arm leaving barely enough room for a plane to come in, drop off canoe paddlers and fly out.

"The first flight was in the cool morning and I had no problem. But at two in the afternoon it was hot and still, without much lift. I came in OK with the empty plane, but flying out I had two canoes, four people and their camping gear. I knew conditions were not good; I should have waited until later, toward evening when it would have cooled off, but I thought I had enough room. In order to get all the takeoff space I could, I taxied north to the wilderness line, right up against the Forest Service sign. Then I swung the nose around to my run south. At this point, Magie flew in with a Cessna 180, taxied over to the west shore and dropped some people off on a campsite. As I shoved the power on, I saw Magie watching from the shore where he had his plane tied up.

"I got the plane off the water but it was not climbing. I could see it was going to be close. The south end of the lake was coming at me fast with its high hills and valley between. I aimed to fly up the valley, but two big pine trees partly blocked the valley entrance. I remembered one of the old pilots telling that once he had to roll his plane sideways to get between those trees. At the last second, I rolled the Beech sideways, went between the trees, climbed out of the valley and headed home.

"Magie flew in behind me and when I got out of the plane I walked over to him and said, 'I just did something stupid! I should never have tried to fly out under the circumstances.'

"Magie didn't bat an eye. He just looked at me. Then a little later he said, 'How would you like to fly a trip to the Arctic?' He had that kind of confidence in his pilots. He could size up a situation, know the options and recognize if you had reacted correctly, even in a bad situation.

Gary Mitchell with Cessna

"I was nervous about that Arctic trip when we took off for Mountain Lake, 240 miles northwest of Churchill, on Hudson Bay. Because fuel could be a problem in that huge, sparse country, I questioned all the Canadian operators I met and learned the locations of several remote fuel caches in addition to villages and regular gas stops. All the Canadians asked was that if I took some of their fuel, I would pay for it and let them know how much I took so they could replace it on another flight.

"North of Red Lake we ran into some bad weather and I turned around, heading back in the rain. The fuel warning light had come on as we dropped into a lake with a fuel cache and a trapper's cabin where we hoped to spend the night. After we tied up, two of the passengers launched a canoe and went fishing while I tried to get the cabin in shape. It had a mud floor and the roof leaked badly, not good accommodations. About then, the two fishermen came back to report they had spotted a vacant Canadian tent camp just up the lake, so we loaded up and taxied to the camp where we spent a comfortable night.

"Next afternoon we flew to a Hudson Bay Post on Island Lake and not far down the lake was the village of Emilie where we loaded up with gas. Next we flew in rain to Ilford on the railroad from Winnipeg to Churchill where we picked up fishing licenses for two of the anglers. The weather remained poor so I put the fishermen up in a little hotel for the night and I slept in the plane. Next day was clear and we flew to an Arctic lake where we enjoyed several days of great fishing for trout and grayling. Our flight back was uneventful, and a little later Magie had me fly some hunters north for goose shooting.

"We had an accident at Big Trout Lake when we were trying to tie up. The dock was jammed with Canadian planes, but there was a space big enough to fit in the Twin Beech if we slipped in sideways. The wind was blowing in, which made it tricky getting between the other planes. As we closed in on the dock, I had one of the hunters jump out to catch the pontoon so it wouldn't slam into the timbers. He slipped and his foot got crunched between the dock and the float.

"A doctor in camp gave him first aid and the next day we flew to Big Trout where there was a Canadian medical station and X-ray equipment. The foot wasn't broken and the hunters insisted we continue on to the goose grounds near Severn where we had three days of great shooting."

The incident that revealed a lot about his courage and character occurred in late fall of 1977 when Gary and his friend Don Dorweiler made a canoe trip up the Lake One-Two-Three-Four Chain to Hudson Lake for some walleye fishing. At that time, motors were still legal in the Boundary Waters Wilderness, which allowed them to travel with a Grumman 17-foot square stern canoe and three-horse outboard. The trip was uneventful on the way to Hudson where they picked out a nice campsite, erected their tent and prepared for some pike and walleye fishing. This late in the fall, both the air and water were quite cold and they wore floatation vests as a precaution.

The fish were cooperative and Gary immediately connected with a large pike. Don was in the stern with the landing net and carefully Gary brought the fish around. As Don swept it up in the mesh, the pike made a lurch and the canoe rolled over. The water was numbing, but they were not too far from shore, so Gary did not panic. He first thought they could swim in, hanging onto the canoe. However, after several minutes, it became apparent that the swamped canoe was too unmanageable. The icy water was effectively slowing them down. Gary told Don they would have to abandon their canoe and strike out for shore. Don said he couldn't swim and was fearful of releasing his grip.

Thinking quickly, Gary grabbed a partially-empty outboard gas can, dumped out the remaining fuel and told Don to use the empty can for a float, which, combined with his life jacket, would enable him to swim in. Don steadfastly refused. Gary knew they now had precious little time before hypothermia would paralyze and kill them. He told Don to just float and he would tow him to shore. Don seemed irrational and fought him off. Gary realized they simply had to get out of the ice water and told Don he was heading for shore and to follow him. Don mumbled something but refused to follow. When he hit the bank, Gary stumbled up on the rocks, looked back and saw Don drifting in his life jacket, slumped over. Gary yelled again and again but there was no reply. The problem was further complicated by the fact that their camp with dry clothes, food and matches was on the opposite shore. Gary remembered that when they canoed in, they had seen a group of fishermen planning to set up camp on nearby Lake Four, so he headed through the woods to seek help. The walking helped warm him somewhat, but he saw no sign of the other fishermen.

He realized there was nothing he could do for Don, whom he assumed had died, so he built a shelter from balsam boughs and brush, and crawled in for the night. The next day he started back toward civilization by following the lake shores. The Lake One-to-Four area is a huge, meandering cluster of connecting waterways with numerous deep bays and long points.

Although their map was in the tackle box with the swamped canoe, Gary had flown over the area a number of times and had a mental picture of how the lakes were situated and began the long walk out. At a rest, he discovered a book of paper matches in his shirt pocket. "The walking had dried out my shirt and the matches looked OK so I tried to light them," he recalled. "They would spark and smoke but would not flare up. They were useless."

Gary Mitchell (l) and Lee Schumacher with fish

On foot, he continued toward his destination—Kawishiwi Lodge on Lake One, the only resort in the area. While just ten miles away by water, it was over three times that far through the thick forest, around swamps, over high granite ridges and skirting meandering bays and swamps. But Gary knew if he followed the lake shores he would eventually arrive at the lodge on Lake One at the end of County Road 18 and the lodge had a telephone. So he began walking the shore of Lake Four heading toward Lake Three. What Gary unfortunately did not know was that their camp and swamped canoe had been discovered by another canoe party passing through Hudson and had reported the matter to the authorities. The Lake County Sheriff immediately authorized a search and a floatplane went out from Pat Magie's seaplane base where Gary worked.

Gary was making his way through heavy woods when he heard the drone of the search plane coming. He ran to the highest point he could find only to see the plane go past, heading for Hudson Lake.

"The plane was so close I could see the pilot's face, but he didn't see me," Gary said. "It was terribly disappointing."

The pilot, of course, was looking for the canoe and the fishermen at Hudson, not knowing Gary had now been making his way several miles through the forest. Gary continued onward toward the highway, making another shelter and spending another night in the woods. He was in excellent physical condition and although he had nothing to eat, had plenty of lake water to drink.

Another day came and went and another plane went over carrying searchers. Gary tried using a T-shirt on the end of a pole to attract the pilot's attention but without luck. He continued walking in a northerly direction. The searchers had retrieved Don's body, the canoe and the camp. They had scoured the area but found no trace of Gary and assumed he was in the bottom of the Hudson Lake.

By now, Gary was becoming terribly fatigued. His feet were swollen, making it difficult to walk. By the sixth day, he could only move about 50 paces at a time without stopping to rest. "I had determined that I was going to walk out," he said. "I kept one thing in my mind. That my wife and daughter were back home waiting for me. I fixed on that single thought and I prayed for strength."

He stumbled out on the shore of what he assumed was Lake One. As he worked slowly along the shore, he spotted a boat channel marker and his spirits went up. Then, not far away across the water, he heard the sound of someone hammering. Through the trees he could see the corner of a log building. At this he shouted as loud as he could and the hammering ceased. A figure appeared on the shore across the bay and Gary yelled some more and waved his arms. It was the lodge owner, Dr. Frank Udovich, who was covering the windows and closing the cabins for the winter. In a few moments, Dr. Udovich came across the bay in his boat but stopped a short distance off shore, eyeing Gary with suspicion.

"I must have looked pretty wild," Gary confessed. "I hadn't shaved for a week and my clothes were ragged and muddy. Frank wanted to know what I was doing on the lake shore, and I finally I convinced him who I was and what had happened. He landed, I got in the boat and he took me to the lodge where there was a warm fire and food.

"He really didn't have a whole lot of food left, since he was closing down, but he opened a can of Dinty Moore Beef Stew and

I ate the whole can."

As we sat in the café, Gary took another sip of tea. "The hammering I heard was Doc Udovich boarding up the last cabin for the winter. It was his final day at the lodge. It was that close."

I finished off my tea and studied this husky ex-pilot who related such an experience in a calm, almost matter-of-fact manner. "You exhibited incredible endurance," I observed.

Gary looked at me and looked away. "I never stopped thinking about my wife and my daughter," he said. "And I had my faith. No matter how bad it got, I never once doubted that I would somehow get out."

There is a saying among old-timers who have faced sickness, injury and terrible odds in the wilderness and survived: "A man who won't quit can't be defeated."

Gary Mitchell is living proof.

EMERGENCY *on* FLOATS
BY BOB CARY

$\mathcal{T}$om Harristhal was a Boy Scout leader who headed up a number of canoe trips into the Boundary Waters. Eventually he purchased my Canadian Border Outfitters base on Moose Lake, but in the early years he outfitted with Bill Rom's Canoe Country Outfitters. During a canoe venture to Cherry Lake, near the Gunflint Trail area, Tom had one Scout who thought he was a mountain climber and began scaling a cliff overlooking the lake. The Scout slipped and fell onto some rocks, knocking himself unconscious. In addition, the young man was oozing blood from his ears. Fearing a broken neck or skull fracture, Tom saw that the young man was immobilized, then paddled back to where he could report the accident to Canoe Country Outfitters.

Tom had left word with the Scouts who remained with the injured boy that if help did not come until after dark to set several fires along the shore of Cherry Lake to guide the rescuers in.

"Pat Magie was working for me at the time," noted Rom, "and had purchased a Cessna 180. He volunteered to go after the injured Scout along with Doc Ciriacy who always had a bag packed and ready for emergencies."

By the time the rescue team flew to Cherry Lake, it was nearly midnight and the forest below was black as a bottomless pit. True to Harristhal's instructions, the Scouts lit several fires along the shore of Cherry Lake, giving the pilot a shoreline location in the darkness. However, Pat felt the lake was not only too small but was bounded by sheer cliffs and the margin for error too slim. Instead, he opted to try for Hanson Lake with a larger expanse of water, just over a high ridge from Cherry.

"I had been over that area and guided canoe trips into that area for several years and knew just about the exact location of

78

Hanson Lake, even in the darkness," Magie explained. "I lined up with Cherry Lake, made a few passes to fix the location, then came around several hundred yards east and made several passes where I though Hanson Lake should be, lined up, throttled back, then began letting down into the dark."

Magie's eyes narrowed as he thought back on that night. "Doc and I held our breath as we dropped down into the pitch black, wondering if there would be a lake below or a jumble of tree trunks crashing through the fuselage. When water showed beneath our landing lights, we both started to breathe again."

They taxied to the bank, located the portage to Cherry Lake, hiked across and came out on the shore. Calling across the water, they summoned the Scouts to bring a canoe and paddled to the campsite. Doc checked the young man who had suffered severe spinal injuries in the fall. He gave as much emergency first aid as possible to stabilize the victim, then, with help from the other Scouts, transported him across the portage to the plane, loaded up and flew back to Ely. There was no question in anyone's mind that Magie's flight into Hanson Lake in the dark and Doc Ciriacy's skill saved the life of the Scout.

A Cessna on shore for winter

EMERGENCY on ICE

BY BOB CARY

It was no day to be flying. A nasty northwest wind whipped across the snowdrifted landscape, gusting over 40 miles per hour on a bitter cold spring day in 1970. The seaplane base on Shagawa Lake was buttoned up although the east-west runway on the ice was fairly open. At Vermilion Community College, atop the high hill overlooking the Lake, a construction crew was finishing laying a cement block wall for the new gymnasium. The workmen were in the lee of the wall mixing cement when a horrendous gust hit the site and the new wall collapsed on top of the workmen.

The first indication there was going to be a flying problem was when seaplane base owner Pat Magie called bush pilot Carlo Palombi and told him to get down to the base pronto. An ambulance was bringing a seriously injured workman to the dock and Carlo was needed to fly the victim to the trauma center in Duluth. Carlo and the ambulance arrived at the dock about the same time, the victim accompanied by senior nurse Peg Likar. Peg was monitoring the unconscious patient trying to keep him stable. Peg was also six months pregnant.

"The only plane we had available that would accommodate a stretcher was a Cessna 206 on wheels," Carlo recalled. "We loaded in the victim, Peg climbed alongside and I got set to take off. The wind was gusting so terribly we needed three men to steady the wings to keep the 206 from flipping over on its back as we taxied to the runway and started down the ice. It was a wild ride from the moment we got into the air. The patient was in a lot of trouble with bleeding and labored breathing through a tracheotomy tube, but he was strapped in. Peg was continually working on him, much of the time with her seat belt off. The wind hurled the plane all around the sky and poor Peg gripped the stretcher and braced

80

her hands against the cabin walls to keep from getting bounced all over. On top of that, her pregnancy made her sick most of the way. We flew into the Duluth International Airport, got down on the runway and taxied up to the terminal. A crew of EMTs was waiting for us. They hustled the stretcher out of the plane, into an ambulance and tore out for the hospital. With that done, I took a look at Peg who looked pretty worn from her ordeal. I suggested we go into the lunchroom at the terminal and get two cups of hot coffee.

"Peg was ready for a break after the wild plane ride but too sick to drink coffee. I climbed the stairs to the coffee shop, went in, settled down and ordered. I had just started to drink my coffee when I was paged over the intercom," Carlo recalled. "Wondering what was going on, I got to a phone and was informed by Magie that they had discovered a second injured workman buried in the rubble at the school. Magie said to hurry back to Ely, pick up the second victim and fly him to Duluth. So much for the coffee."

Carlo Palombi

Carlo and Peg raced down to the 206, rode back to Ely and fought the gusts down to the ice runway. At the hangar, a second ambulance with EMTs was waiting. The stretcher was loaded into the 206, and strapped down. Carlo was again guided out to the ice runway by crewmen holding the wing tips. He revved up the engine and took off for a repeat of the first trip with Peg trying to brace herself in the back where she could monitor the victim and still keep from getting banged around inside the cabin. Gusts jerked the light aircraft up, down and sideways.

"We were met the Duluth Airport by another ambulance, unloaded our patient and this time we really had our coffee before heading back to Ely. At least on the return trip Peg had a seat and a seat belt."

Carlo thought for a moment and added, "If they ever gave out Congressional Medals of Honor to civilians, Peg should have gotten one for what she did in the line of duty that day."

NOT SUCH A BAD LANDING

BY BOB CARY

*M*aster Sergeant Claude Taylor, United States Marine Corps, came home from the service at the end of World War II somewhat worse for wear. After fighting for months in the Philippines, Claude was one of the unlucky Marines captured by the Japanese on Bataan and was included in the infamous "Death March" to a prison camp. When he finally returned home to Ely for some needed rest and rehab, he took flying lessons under the G.I. Bill. When he soloed, it was winter and the planes were flying off the ice. One cold day, Claude rented a Cessna 172 and flew to International Falls, just to log some air time. Unfortunately, before he could fly back a howling storm came in from the north. The plowed runway on the lake ran east and west making it impossible for the inexperienced flier to land with such a crosswind. Carlo Palombi was on duty and realized Claude was in a lot of trouble. He called Claude on the radio and told him to keep flying south while he found a place for him to land. Carlo checked on Eveleth, but the only runway open was east-west, which again meant Claude would have to make an impossible landing into the severe cross wind.

"Finally we told Claude the only place he could possibly land was at the Duluth International Airport sixty miles south," noted Carlo. "Claude said he had never landed at a regular airport and didn't know the procedure.

"Gary Mitchell and I went up in a 180 and caught up with Claude coming down from International Falls, and we told him to follow us to Duluth. Even with good radio contact, Gary and I were really worried, but we guided Claude to the Duluth Airport and then 'talked him down' in the howling wind to the runway without a hitch. We climbed out of our plane pretty shaky, but

83

Claude got out of his plane, cool as could be, like he did it every day."

Carlo thought a minute. "I guess after the Bataan Death March there was not a whole lot that was going to upset Claude."

Leithold Seaplane Service advertisement

CLOSE CALLS & BAD ENDS

"Some old pilots point out that there are two kinds of luck: good and bad. And if you are going to have some, it is best to have the good kind."

WHEN FEAR IS *a* CO-PILOT BY JACK HAUTALA

*D*o pilots hear things in the air, things like music? I was reading a book about women pilots who flew in World War II and was surprised to learn that one admitted she heard music while she flew. I thought I was the only one who heard music when flying, but maybe some just don't want to admit it. Yes, I hear music when flying serenely high over the earth. But I don't recall hearing music when things were going wrong and the situation was getting tense. There is a great feeling of relief, even euphoria, that sets in after a tough flight when life may have been hanging by a thread of pure luck.

I read about a pilot who talked about how his body would shake when he got into a very dangerous situation, when things were so bad he realized he might not make it. Not many pilots are honest enough to admit this, but I think it happens more than most let on. All pilots like to give the impression that they handled every tight situation in a cool, resourceful manner, totally in control. And most of the time this is true. But there are times when a situation arises that forces a pilot to recognize disaster is imminent, when terror creeps into the cockpit. What separates the experienced bush pilot from the unlucky ones is the ability to keep functioning and flying when scared witless.

One moose hunting season my hunting companion and I were camped on the shore of a very small tree-rimmed Ontario lake. Late in the second day, we scored on a big bull, which we promptly dressed out. We cut the huge animal into quarters and muscled the quarters up the floats of my Cessna 180 and into the plane. Then we washed the blood off our hands, loaded in our camping gear, pushed the plane loose from the shore, climbed into the cabin and prepared to take off. It had not been particularly difficult flying over the spruce trees into that little lake when we came there, but my instincts told me that with several hundred pounds of moose meat on board, along with guns and camping gear, things were apt to be tight getting out. In addition, it was a damp fall day with little wind and not much lift to help us.

Missed water, hit land

Not willing to risk everything on one chance, I twice taxied down the lake, gunned the throttle and circled on one float to get up speed. On the second try, we achieved a lift-off, but there was not enough room to get out. As I cut the throttle for another try, the plane leaped into the air, which got real exciting with the end of the lake coming up. Luckily, I was able to stop before we went into the shore. After two tries, and one lift off, I felt we were ready. I taxied the 180 as close to shore as possible and started another run into the wind.

As soon as we lifted off I knew it was going to be close, tree-touching close. The plane was climbing very slowly, and the spruce trees were coming at us very fast. I could achieve climb only if I held the flaps at 14 degrees, which is between the notches on the flap control. Thus, I had to hold it in position with my right hand on the flap handle. At the same time, I was gripping the vertical and horizontal control wheel with my left hand. To make sure I had full throttle and prop control, I was jerking my hand from the control wheel to slam those buttons to the firewall or beyond. I realized I was running out of hands, but by then we were at the end of the lake and I was shaking so bad my feet were doing a dance on the rudder pedals. At the last second, the Cessna took us out of there, moose and all, just barely over the trees and into clear sky. A great sense of relief and thankfulness swept over me and the music started playing in my head.

When we got back to Ely, we unloaded the plane and stacked the meat where it would stay cool until we could get it to the butcher shop. When I got home for supper I related to my brother Wiley the day's adventures. Wiley looked at me in his usual unperturbed manner, and drily asked why I hadn't simply made a couple of trips, flying half the moose at a time out to a bigger lake nearby, where there was plenty of room for a takeoff with the whole load. As I stood there wondering why I hadn't thought of that, I realized that not exploring all my options had nearly cost me, and the music I might have been hearing would have been something like "When the Saints Go Marching In."

THE COWBOY

BY BOB CARY & JACK HAUTALA

 $\mathcal{B}$ oth of us were involved with this pilot and both have different pieces of the story.

Hautala: From 1952, when the federal air ban went into effect over the Boundary Waters, to 1965, there was very little flying. However, by 1965, Pat Magie had figured out how to land in periphery lakes around the rim of the wilderness, offering access to canoe fishermen. He also acquired a Canadian permit so he could fly into the mass of lakes outside Quetico Provincial Park in Ontario, plus other areas farther north to Hudson Bay. Magie opened up a floatplane operation at Sandy Point on Shagawa Lake, called Wilderness Wings.

Cary: This coincided with my starting up Canadian Border Outfitters on Moose Lake in 1966, and we immediately teamed up with Magie to fly canoe groups and equipment to remote lakes from whence they would paddle the lake chains back to our base. Local wags like Danny Peterson and Jim Beatty, who worked at my canoe base at the time, quickly changed the name of Wilderness Wings to "Wiggly Wings," although it was one of the safest bush operations anywhere and had some of the finest floatplane pilots that ever cracked open a throttle in North America. With a couple of exceptions and one of these was The Cowboy.

Hautala: When Magie's flying business began to boom he needed more experienced pilots because most of us were flying from daylight to dark and sometimes into the dark. Magie ran ads in the aviation magazines looking for fliers. One pilot who sent in an impressive resume was named Jay Alfred, who claimed to have a considerable wealth of experience flying in Alaska. Magie hired him and Jay came in to work.

Cary: The first time I met The Cowboy, he was sitting on the pontoons of a Cessna 180 floating in the middle of the bay adjacent to my canoe base. I was doing some dock repair and had a party of two with one canoe and gear standing by, scheduled for a flight to Lac La Croix. It looked like one of Magie's planes in the bay, so I hopped in a boat and motored out. The pilot sitting on the floats had been studying a map and glanced up. "Do you know where Canadian Border Outfitters is?" he asked.

"Yeah, It's my place," I said. "Just follow the boat back."

I tied the boat as he taxied up and we hooked bow and stern lines to the dock from pontoon cleats on the left side. "The people are packed and ready to fly to Lac La Croix," I noted.

Flying a canoe party in

"Yeah?" he muttered. "Where is Lac La Croix?"

A little twinge of warning shot through my mind as I got out a couple of large scale maps and marked the route down the Basswood River through Crooked Lake to Iron Lake and La Croix, about a 45 minute ride including a stop at the Canadian customs on Basswood Lake. I marked Basswood Falls, Curtain Falls and Rebecca Falls on the map as landmarks easily seen from the air. That done, we loaded the people and their gear into the Cessna and flipped their canoe upside down up on the floats. It immediately became apparent that Jay Alfred had no idea how to rope a canoe to a pontoon. It isn't a complicated process, but it has to be done right with the ropes cinched down so the canoe cannot wobble or seesaw and possibly come loose and tear the tail section off the plane. So I lashed the canoe onto the float and the plane took off. I promptly went inside and phoned Magie at Wilderness Wings. "That new pilot got lost just coming out here from town," I noted. "And he's got some other problems."

"How's that?"

"Listen. He doesn't know where Lac La Croix is located and he couldn't tie a canoe on the floats. This guy is spooky."

"He's new," Magie said. "I'll keep an eye on him."

Hautala: The old pilots were wary of Jay Alfred. He could fly but he didn't seem to have much knowledge of floatplanes or much common sense. And he flew sort of heavy-handed. In short order he got the nickname 'Cowboy' and it stuck. One of our regular drops was at Murphy Lake, a small, narrow piece of water on the rim of the wilderness, offering canoe access to Horse Lake, Horse River and unlimited waters beyond. The pickup point for guests was a campsite halfway up the west shore. Regular procedure was to pick up the people, taxi to the far north end of the lake and take off with plenty of lake ahead because there were some big hills on the south end of the lake.

The Cowboy flew in one evening to pick up some fishermen and fly them back to Ely. Unfortunately, he decided to take off from the middle of the lake and as he flew toward the north end realized he couldn't get enough altitude to clear the hills. In desperation he attempted to bank and come back south but hooked a wing tip and cartwheeled into the lake. Luckily, no one was hurt in the crash but the Cessna was a wreck.

He figured he had better not show up at Wilderness Wings again and he left town in a hurry. Magie filed a complaint with the FAA and tried to get The Cowboy's license pulled but with no luck. Jay Alfred returned to Alaska and began flying again, where his career ended in a fatal crash.

FEARLESS TONY

BY JACK HAUTALA

*T*ony Massaro was short, muscular and had been a star hockey player in the Canadian leagues. In the 1960s, Tony opened a resort on Powell Lake, just east of Quetico Provincial Park, providing comfortable accommodations and access to excellent fishing, not only at Powell but also at nearby Clay and Mack Lakes. The Powell Lake area was full of trophy moose, and the Ontario record was taken by hunters near the camp. His camp was also a preferred drop-off spot for canoe paddlers who would leave from Clay Lake and paddle down the Wawiag River to Kawnipi and thence back to the outfitting complexes on the U.S. side of the Boundary Waters. One of Tony's daredevil tricks was to race down the twisty, log-filled river from Powell to Mack Lake wide open in his outboard boat. He scared the pants off some of his guests, but he was fearless and confident of his ability.

Tony annually attended a number of U.S. sport shows where he made contact with fishermen and hunters who increasingly booked trips to his resort. It looked like he had everything working for him when misfortune lay a heavy hand on his life. Tony's wife and young daughter lived at the camp in the summer and the child was as fearless as her father. She loved to race her bicycle around the camp and down to the waterfront. One day she ran her bike down the dock and into the lake, where she drowned. Tony and his wife were heartbroken and the grieving mother refused to live in the camp any longer, moved to Thunder Bay and came back only occasionally to visit.

Tony determined to keep operating. Since there was no road into the camp, he maintained close contact with the floatplane operators who brought in guests and supplies. When he needed to go to town, he would hitch a ride with one of the planes returning empty to Ely.

One Friday night when Tony was scheduled to fly with me, it was already getting late when I dropped in to pick him up. I kept trying to hurry him along but he told me not to worry because he knew the country like the back of his hand, even in the dark. Just as night settled in, we took off, climbed to 4000 feet and headed for Ely on instruments. Tony was looking out the window and after a bit murmured, "It's sure dark out there, isn't it?"

Pitch dark. The only thing we could see was the glow of the instrument panel. After a half hour of flying through the black night, distant bright lights on Ely's football stadium came into view, guiding us to town, and we landed at the Sandy Point base without incident. Tony had been very quiet on the trip, and I am sure he began to realize how dark the northwoods could be at night.

A plane crash in a backyard in Ely

Tony Massaro's business expanded to where he felt he needed a floatplane of his own instead of relying on commercial pilots all the time. He purchased a Cub Coupe, a nice little two-place aircraft he used for fishing and hunting. One winter day, when Tony's wife and two friends were visiting, the three men decided to fly from Powell to nearby Red Fox Lake, noted for a nice population of lake trout. Since the Cub Coupe was a two-place plane, it meant two trips to get all three of them into Red Fox unless they could somehow squeeze all of them aboard. The Coupe had been known to sometimes handle three passengers, but extreme care had to be taken with this much load. Tony's wife was watching from the lodge window as all three climbed into the cab and taxied down the ice. With full throttle, the skis cleared the surface and things looked all right but the aircraft was not climbing fast enough to clear the trees at the end of the lake. In desperation, Tony banked and turned back but lost speed, and as he cut past the front of the lodge, the plane stalled and went straight into the ice killing all three of them in plain view of his horrified wife. There are people who say you go when your time is up. Maybe fearless Tony's time was just running out. Only the two fishermen who climbed in the plane with him didn't know that.

Fatal crash near Duluth

LUCK

BY BOB CARY

$\mathcal{S}$ome old pilots point out that there are two kinds of luck: good and bad. And if you are going to have some, it is best to have the good kind.

Joe Pucel Jr. had a lot going for him. He was the successful owner and manager of the IGA supermarket in Ely, beloved as a family man, civic leader, a veteran outdoorsman and an accomplished private pilot. Once, coming back on a trip from Canada, he ran out of gas just south of Murphy Lake, and made a perfect landing in a small beaver pond. The plane was later flown out.

Joe Pucel's plane after the wreck near Big Moose Lake

One day Joe was flying with his son Jamie and State Rep. Dave Battaglia, heading toward Crane Lake. They were following the Echo Trail Corridor, a legal flight lane between the north and south segments of the federal wilderness.

Just past Big Lake, the engine on the Cessna 185 conked out and Joe aimed for an emergency landing on Big Moose Lake, a short distance away. He coolly nursed the crippled bird over the trees toward the water and tersely ordered Jamie and Dave to be ready and flip off their seat belts when they hit the lake in order to exit the plane quickly.

A few hundred yards from the lake, a single big tree loomed up in their flight path sending them crashing into the woods. Jamie came out of the wreck with minor injuries. Rep. Battaglia was seriously injured and Joe was killed. The shocked town of Ely mourned the loss of a much respected citizen.

"IT WAS *a* DARK *and* STORMY NIGHT"   BY JACK HAUTALA

*O*ne summer day, Wiley and I flew a couple of vacationing businessmen to Illinois for a quick trip, intending to fly them back to Ely the same night. I was instructing Wiley on instrument flying and the flight afforded good conditions for training. We were in Magie's new Cessna Cardinal that accommodated four of us comfortably. It was fast and had good radios. I filed a flight plan and off we went to Champaign, Illinois. The flight was uneventful and after dropping off our passengers, we had the day to kill. Since Champaign is a college town, it was easy to spend the day watching all the people strolling by.

When the time for the flight back to Ely approached, I filed an IFR flight plan with Air Traffic Control and checked with the passengers to see if the departure time was still OK. They said there would be a delay for about an hour, which required a change in the flight plan.

We took off in the evening, planning to arrive in Ely at 11 p.m. Things went smoothly until we reached Hinckley, Minnesota, when we were informed by radio that a squall line was in our path and what did we intend to do about it? I told Traffic Control we would try a lower altitude and look at the storm to see if we could get under it. That was a big mistake, but in the dark it was hard to judge the strength of the squall. As we hit the front we almost rolled over a few times and beat a hasty retreat. I called ATC and told them we would need clearance to divert west around the front toward Brainerd, then on to Hibbing and then to Ely.

About 10 miles from Hibbing, ATC informed us that the storm passing through the area had knocked out the runway lights at Hibbing, Duluth and Ely and what was our next move? They had no information on Eveleth so I told him we would head for

Eveleth to see if they had any lights. The weather was slowly improving and when we came in over Eveleth, we spotted the runway lights and landed. We filled the plane with gas and phoned Ely to have someone drive down to Eveleth and pick up our passengers, then we would see about getting the plane back home. The two businessmen said they would go on with us, but I told them it was too chancy and we might end up in Minneapolis for the night. At 11:30 we taxied out and took off into clearing skies and I thought the worst was behind us. But just as we lifted off we saw fog forming rapidly over the ground.

We flew on to Ely hoping we would find a hole over the airport and get down; if not, we could fly to Minneapolis. It was a weird night with the ground white below and the stars out up above. Arriving over Ely, we saw the red light on top of the airport VOR and dim lights of the parking lot but nothing else. We circled around and tried a normal VOR approach, dropping down to 200 feet, but we could not see the runway with our landing lights.

We tried this six more times, when suddenly Wiley said: "There it is" and pointed to a small strip of white line on the wet, black runway. I throttled down, and as a precaution, I decided to land with the brakes on so when we hit, our roll would be kept to a minimum. We knew we were over the runway, but we had no idea what part of the runway and how close we were to the end. We picked out a bit of white line on the blacktop and dropped down holding our breath. It worked and we stopped short of the woods.

There's an old story that starts out: "It was a dark and stormy night." Wiley and I were in it and we had just one aim: to get the plane down and on the ground intact. With a little luck, we made it.

FOGGY FLYING BY JACK HAUTALA

*O*nce, leaving on a night trip back from Powell Lake, I noticed the smaller lakes were strangely turning fluffy white. After a few minutes, I realized that it was fog, an ominous sign. The bigger lakes were still fairly clear but obviously not for long. In addition, I was cutting it pretty short on fuel and didn't have a lot of extra time. Basswood Lake was fairly clear as I came over so I aimed for Shagawa, determined that if it was fogged over, I would head straight back to Basswood, land and tie up to the shore for the night. As I approached Shagawa, it was a relief to see it was still open. I made a glassy water landing, taxied to the dock and tied up. By the time I had all the lines tied to the dock, fog was rolling in and within five minutes I had a difficult time seeing well enough to drive my car to town. It was that quick. And this is as close as a pilot could push his luck and still make it.

Planes on Crooked Lake

101

HUMOR & INGENUITY

"Perhaps it is the life they lead, pretty much on the edge or possibly a little over the edge..."

TRICKS

*P*erhaps it is the life they lead, pretty much on the edge or possibly a little over the edge, but bush pilots have a keen sense of humor. Some are subdued and ironic. Some uproarious. But they all appreciate a good laugh.

When Ely businessman Joe Debeltz was building his cabin up on Wolf Lake, just north of Tower, it was in a remote area where the only good access was by floatplane. So he had all the building material flown in. This included concrete blocks, bags of cement, roofing and logs cut to size for the walls. The work horse for this endeavor was a twin-engine Beech 18 flying out of Wilderness Wings.

Once Carlo Palombi was flying a load of building supplies in with Joe and his son as passengers. It was one of those humdrum days, quiet, sunshiny, pretty boring. Joe Debeltz had fallen asleep, sagging against his seat belt, his head resting on his chest. Carlo got an urge to liven up the proceedings a trifle and caught the attention of the younger Debeltz. Carlo indicated he was going to do something. He shut down one of the two engines on the Twin Beech.

"It flew well on one engine and I had plenty of room," Carlo recalled. "We were over big Lake Vermilion with lots of water to land on if I needed it."

He signaled the son to wake up his dad, which he did. And pointed out the window at the engine with the feathered prop.

"Joe Debeltz," Carlo noted, "went ballistic. He thought we were about to crash. After a minute, I turned the power back on and we finished our flight. I don't think Debeltz ever took a nap in a plane again."

COOLING OFF *the* HOT SHOT

BY BOB CARY

*O*nce a young, new pilot was hired on at Wilderness Wings Airways. Although having limited experience, he carried on like he was the greatest flier in the world. Pat Magie was looking for some way to cool the jets on this Hot Shot, bring him back to reality. One of the less desirable flying jobs bush pilots were forced to accept was flying the occasional deceased person back to their home town. On rare instances, someone visiting in Ely would suffer a heart attack or some other fatal occurrence, and it fell upon the air service to transport the remains.

Thus it was one warm and sunshiny day that the Hot Shot arrived at the base to witness Magie and some crew members loading a heavy body bag onto the co-pilot seat of a 180 Cessna. Magie summoned the Hot Shot, pointed to the bag and said the mortal remains were to be delivered to a lake in southern Minnesota. With obvious distaste for the mission the Hot Shot climbed into the cabin of the 180, turned over the prop, taxied down the lake and took off.

Inside the control shack, the crew listened intently as the pilot reported his heading and air speed. Then the radio went silent. But only for a minute. The Hot Shot came back on the radio with a somewhat strained whisper.

"I don't think the body in the bag is really dead," he said.

"Whatta you mean," Magie shot back.

"Listen, I tell you he's not dead. He just groaned."

"Oh, come on," Magie chided. "The doctor signed the death certificate. He was already stiff when we loaded him into the plane."

Another minute went by and the Hot Shot's voice came back on the radio, this time with a definite note of panic. "He just groaned again. I heard him real plain. The guy in the bag isn't dead."

"Listen," Magie said, "don't give us that stuff. You've got a corpse in a body bag. Just fly him down to Minneapolis."

The next emission from the Hot Shot was high pitched, bordering on hysteria. "He not only groaned, he moved! This guy is certainly not dead!" There was sheer terror in his voice. "I'm turning around and heading straight back!"

Two minutes later, the plane came in, made a rather abrupt approach, landed and taxied at high speed to the dock. Magie grabbed the wing as the door banged open and the Hot Shot leaped out, ran up the gravel by the radio shack and stood wild-eyed, hands on hips.

"What's the matter with you?" Magie yelled.

"He's not dead!" the Hot Shot yelled back.

Magie and another crewmen lifted the body bag out of the plane and laid it gently on the dock. "This corpse isn't groaning," Magie said.

The Hot Shot took a couple of steps toward the dock as Magie grabbed the zipper tab and unzipped the bag. A grinning 'corpse' climbed out—another pilot. "He was going nuts!" the corpse laughed. Then they all laughed. Even the Hot Shot laughed. He went on to become an accomplished pilot, although a somewhat less pretentious one.

Loading a Norseman for a trip north

106

FUNNY LANDINGS

BY JACK HAUTALA

Ed Junke, from Ely, was taking off from Murphy Lake in his Cessna 172 with several passengers on board. As he approached the south end of the lake, he realized he might not clear the trees, hauled the wheel back to gain a little more altitude, stalled and went down nose-first. Instead of smashing into the rocks, however, the plane caught in the trees and ended up suspended upside down with the prop not even touching the ground. Ed and his friends scrambled out, nobody injured.

One dead still day, Mike Tappa and I were flying up to Stormy Lake and as we were climbing out of the Canadian customs station at Rainy Lake, we saw a duck below us that seemed to be having difficulty trying to land on the glassy water. Every now and then he would stop flapping his wings and set up to land, figuring he was close to the water. Unfortunately, he was still about ten feet up and apparently couldn't judge the distance. Finally he stopped flapping, dropped down with a big splash and rolled over a few times. Even expert fliers sometimes have trouble with glassy water landings.

I saw Clinton Smith do the same thing one day landing on Rolando's Bay in Shagawa Lake near the Forest Service hangar. He was coming in from the north for a glassy water landing but was carrying too much power. As he entered the bay, he was still ten feet above the surface and not slowing down. The end of the bay was coming fast, so he cut the power and dropped the last ten feet with a huge splash. The plane came to a stop just short of the hangar.

FLIGHT INSTRUCTION
BY BOB CARY

$\mathcal{O}$ne of the perennial stories of the old, "old" days involved an enterprising young citizen named Tom Harri. The Harri family was quite large and rather prominent in and around Ely, known as solid, industrious folk.

Young Tom was, among other things, an excellent mechanic, a skill in much demand by floatplane operators. He repaired and tuned up aircraft engines for all the major operators and eventually bought his own plane. Just bought it. Didn't fly it. Didn't know how to fly. He kept it tied to the dock and allowed others to fly it once in a while, fully intending to take lessons and become a pilot. One of the procedures Tom used when tuning up engines was to get in the cockpit, start the engine, open the throttle a bit and taxi around the lake on the floats, sometimes getting up on the step, which is close to getting airborne.

Now the story gets a trifle "iffy" because there are many variations of what occurred, but here is one told to me by John Lobe, an old WWII veteran who was a young man at the time. John and Tom Mooney were hanging around the seaplane base near where Mooney had a small canoe outfitting business. Tom Harri had been tuning up his own plane, climbed out of the cabin and onto a float. "Hey, Mooney!" he yelled. "Want to go for a ride?"

Mooney thought it would be fun to taxi at high speed around the lake on floats and climbed aboard the little aircraft that boasted just two seats, side-by-side. This gave Mooney the thrill of being right up front where he could see everything Harri was doing. Since it was a two-seater, John Lobe was left watching enviously from the dock.

As the engine revved up and they got moving, Tom Harri suddenly asked: "Hey, Mooney, will you reach in and get that little booklet out of the pocket in the door?"

"What booklet?"

"The flight manual."

"What for?" Mooney was beginning to get a little apprehensive.

"Just get it out, put it on your lap and open it up to where it says 'Takeoff and Landing.'"

Although now considerably alarmed, Mooney lay the book on his lap and found the chapter dealing with takeoffs.

"Read what it says," Harri ordered.

Sweating profusely, Mooney slowly read the takeoff procedure. Harri nodded, shoved the throttle forward as they went roaring down the lake, then wobbled off the water and into the air.

"See!" Harri laughed. "I knew I could fly this thing!"

At that point an island loomed up ahead. Harri hauled back slightly on the stick, managed to clear the island, but came down on the other side, hooked a wing and cartwheeled into the lake.

Neither of them was hurt but the plane was a wreck. All of it happened in plain view of a number of townfolk who lived along the shore of Shagawa Lake. Harri went on to take lessons and became a passable pilot. But all anyone remembered was the time he took the plane off with a minimum of skill but a super supply of confidence. Tom Mooney? When they fished him out of the lake, Lobe asked him what went wrong. "We weren't in the air long enough for me to read him the part about landing." Mooney replied.

Bohman Airways plane

ONE THAT BLEW UP

BY JACK HAUTALA

*B*utch Simeske got into flying by way of a stringer of walleyes. A carpenter in Minneapolis, he came north on vacation and was flown into a remote lake by Wilderness Wings. Flown out with his limit of walleyes, Butch decided he wanted to be a bush pilot and began taking lessons in Minneapolis, received his rating and came to Ely as part of Pat Magie's operation.

One day, Butch flew in with a 180 and dropped two people, a canoe and the gear off at Canadian Border Outfitters on Moose Lake. He was supposed to pick up another group, but found that the load was too heavy for the 180. Butch decided to go back for the 206, which could handle the load. He taxied around the corner and took off empty. There is some argument about what happened next, but for some reason, instead of taking the full length of the lake, Butch opened the throttle and buzzed over Bernie Carlson's Quetico-Superior Outfitters and up the big hill behind. The steep angle coupled with low fuel in the tanks caused the engine to quit, and Butch plowed into the trees. The plane smashed through a lot of aspen and birch, came up against a big tree that stopped the plane, slid down the trunk, hit the ground upside down and burst into flame. A Forest Service patrol plane saw the fire and called Magie's base on the radio. They told us no one could have survived the crash. Then Flossie Carlson called to tell us Butch had crashed. Some of Carlson's crew and some of the Canadian Border Outfitters' crew were running up the hill with fire extinguishers. At the crash site, the fire was so intense no one could get close. Everyone assumed Butch was burning up in the plane until someone spotted him standing somewhat dazed at the edge of the woods leaning against a tree, with just a little hair singed off.

Butch said that when the plane hit the ground and flamed up, the doors were jammed shut. In desperation, he kicked out the windshield and scrambled to safety. There was nothing left of the plane except the engine. Even the floats burned.

Butch Simeske flew a few more trips but decided finally to get into some other line of work. I think he went back to being a carpenter in Minneapolis.

Unloading gear at camp

WORLD'S SMALLEST AIRCRAFT CARRIER   BY JACK HAUTALA

*M*y brother Wiley was not only a superb pilot, he was also an excellent mechanic. Dad named him Wiley after the famous race pilot Wiley Post. Beloved American cowboy humorist Will Rogers and Post were making a world tour in a floatplane in 1935 and both were killed on takeoff when the plane dove into the Alaskan tundra near Point Barrow.

Wiley learned to fly from our dad, Ernie, and from dad's good friend Millard Whittig who had a flying school in Hibbing. Millard had several J-3 Cubs he used for flight instruction. One night in a snowstorm, Millard was flying home to Hibbing in a Cessna 195 and was staying down low so he could spot the airport lights when he got close. There was a big, flat swamp south of the airport, which made flying low no problem. Unfortunately, when crossing the swamp, Millard got too low and hit the ground at cruise speed, totaling the plane, himself and two passengers.

One of Wiley's tricks was to toss a roll of toilet paper out of a plane and as it unrolled, see how many times he could cut it with a wing before the roll hit the ground. One winter when he had a Cub on skis, he was flying down Shagawa Lake and spotted a friend racing over the ice in his car. Wiley dropped the Cub down and touched the guy's car roof with his skis. Once I owned a 90-horsepower J-3 Cub and Wiley cut loops with this plane, sometimes coming out no more than 100 feet off the ground.

One winter, Doc Soderberg lost a wheel off his plane making a landing at the Tower Airport. Wiley and I flew over in my Cub on skis, landed on Lake Vermilion and walked across the snow to the runway where we inspected Doc's Cub and decided what has to be done to fix it. When we got back to my plane and tried to take off, we found the snow too deep and sticky. Wiley got out to push on the wing as I gunned the engine to get us rolling, but when I throttled back to let him climb in, the plane stopped. After we tried this a couple of times, Wiley said to keep it at full power and he would climb in as we went. He pushed on the wing until the plane got rolling, then jumped on a ski and rode holding a strut. I picked up speed and he pulled himself into the cab just before I lifted off.

At one point, Wiley owned a Champ and was working on it at the Ely Airport. He installed floats on the plane inside the hangar and then began wondering how to get the plane through town to Shagawa Lake without taking it apart. Tommy Richards had a big flatbed truck and Wiley asked him to bring it to the airport. They skidded the Champ up on the flatbed, Wiley climbed in the plane and Tommy drove the flatbed to the far end of the runway. Then, as Wiley started up the engine on the plane, Tommy roared down the runway, eventually getting it up to 65 miles an hour. At that point, Wiley gunned the Champ, lifted off the flatbed and flew to Shagawa Lake where he landed on the floats.

Wiley patched up and flew home wrecked airplanes no one else would fly. He seemed to know if they would hold together or not and always made it back.

Wiley Hautala

Wiley was also an expert at getting stranded planes out of the woods. Sometimes these planes would be considerably banged up, but Wiley would go in with tubing, sheet metal screws, cables, wire and tools, straighten out the bent elevators or rudders, brace the fuselage with tubing, run cable from the struts to the wings to hold the ship together and fly it out. He checked out one in a small pond near town and the conventional wisdom was that the plane would have to be taken apart and hauled out in pieces. Wiley had the plane stripped down, extra seats taken out and the gas drained with only ten gallons left. He tied the tail of the plane to a tree on shore, started the engine, revved it up until the floats were bouncing up and down on the water, whereupon a helper cut the rope, and Wiley roared out over the trees.

Another time, young Joe Pucel ran out of gas coming back from a Canadian fishing trip and was forced to land in a beaver pond on a creek. There didn't seem to be any way to take off and clear the trees surrounding the pond. Wiley stripped the plane of all extra weight, put in a few gallons of gas, then went upstream on the creek and broke open two other beaver dams. The extra water poured down, enlarging the pond holding the plane, allowing just enough room to fly it out.

One of his jobs was installing floats on wheel planes. People who wanted to fly into the lake country north of Ely would buy wheel planes at an airport and then seek somebody who could put the craft on floats. Getting a plane from the Ely airport down to the waterfront on Shagawa Lake was often quite a chore and might require taking the wings off to truck the fuselage to the lake and install the wings later.

Wiley solved this by landing wheel planes on a little strip of dirt road across the lake from the seaplane base. The usable part of the road, almost on the lake shore, was very short and bordered with trees. There was no room for error. But since the road was dirt, the landing could be made with the brakes locked, coming to a skidding stop and keeping the aircraft from rolling off the road and into the trees.

Although a few other pilots tried it successfully, Wiley was the only person with enough skill to land there regularly. To get a plane from the road over to the hangar at the seaplane base across the lake, Wiley had Rabs Camish build the "aircraft carrier," really a barge, out of 12-inch diameter steel tubing decked with pine planks. A driveway to an old mine water pumping station connected the road to the lake. Planes were taxied on their wheels down the driveway and up a ramp to the aircraft carrier deck. A ten-horse outboard motor powered the whole rig slowly to the seaplane base. It was quite a sight for Ely citizens to see that barge steaming across Shagawa Lake with an airplane riding on the deck.

THE BUSH PILOT'S WIFE

BY BOB CARY

*B*ush pilots are a unique lot, but so are the women who marry them. It has been said by backyard philosophers that all marriage is a crap shoot, and you never know what will turn up until you roll the dice. A lot of the dice turn up snake eyes, at least from the standpoint of the bride, which is why there is a considerable amount of divorce involving women married to men who fly on floats. It takes a strong woman to compete with a pilot's love of planes and flying, and one of the strongest is Doris Hautala.

Doris was married to the late Wiley Hautala, a bush flying legend. Both grew up in Ely and attended school there, and both had a little streak of daredevil in their makeup. Both were talented people—Wiley in flying and aircraft mechanics, Doris in music and the arts. And both had hardy Finnish backgrounds, a plus for those living on the edge of the northern bush where winters are long and summers are short.

"You never knew what Wiley was going to do next," Doris observed. "Once he called the house and said he wanted to take me for a plane ride. This sounded like a good deal until I got in the car and he said he had to stop out at the airport for a minute. Pat Magie, the local Cessna dealer, had sold a wheel plane to a man in Maine and Wiley had the job of delivering it. He said that on the way we could fly over Niagara Falls, which sounded romantic to him, but didn't excite me much. We stopped at Rockford for lunch and I had a hamburger, which was a mistake. Anyway, we did fly over Niagara Falls and then Wiley though it would be neat to fly down the Erie Canal to New York and then up to Maine.

"The problem was, the Erie Canal winds and twists all over, and that's when I realized I never should have eaten that hamburger, because I got sick. I told Wiley I was getting sick and he said to stick my head out the window, don't urp in the plane. Well, you know what happens if you throw something out of a plane window…it comes right back in. I threw up and it blew back all over the inside of the plane; so we had to find an airport, land and spend a lot of time scrubbing out the inside of the plane before he could deliver it to the customer.

"Another time, we flew a plane to a customer in Boston. We delivered the plane and took a rented car to Boston's Logan Airport from where we had tickets to fly back to Minneapolis. However, we missed our connection and couldn't fly out until the next morning. After renting the car, Wiley didn't have any more money. Magie forgot to send along expense money so we couldn't stay at a motel. With nothing else to do, we drove all over Boston the whole night and caught the plane back to Minneapolis as soon as morning came. Magie said he had arranged to have somebody fly down to Minneapolis to meet us, but nobody showed up. Wiley called Ely and found out they were over-booked and had no planes or pilots free. Luckily, we ran into some Ely people at the airport who were driving home and we got a ride back with them. It seemed like things were forever like that.

"Wiley was always calling me up to go some place for lunch, but I never knew where we were going until we got in the plane. Once he picked me up and we went to the Ely Airport where he had been repairing the landing gear on a wheel plane somebody had cracked on a hard landing. At the airport I found out we were going to deliver the repaired plane to St. Paul. Lunch in St. Paul would be fine, I thought, and we were sailing along very smoothly over Route I-35 when suddenly there was no sound. The engine just quit and we had to find a field for an emergency landing. Wiley quickly picked out what looked like a smooth field on a farm next to the highway and dropped in.

"We had only one chance and the field turned out to be a little short. The plane overran the field and we crashed into some trees at the end. Since we were alongside the highway, the accident drew a crowd of onlookers who were attracted to the wreck. We spent some time explaining to these people how we happened to be there.

"Wiley was wondering why the engine quit running and guessed that maybe the first accident jarred something loose, which is why it stopped running just before we reached St. Paul."

They had to stay at the field with the plane until Magie flew another aircraft down to get them. This plane had a problem—the door on the passenger side where Doris was sitting wouldn't stay shut. "I complained to Wiley and he said not to worry. Just hang onto the door so it didn't bang around. He said my seat belt would hold me in the plane O.K. and I wouldn't fall out.

"In lot of ways Wiley was a genius with aircraft," Doris observed. "He could rebuild any plane and knew a lot about floats and how to install them. He was having some problems installing Edo floats on some of the planes and determined the company didn't have them rigged out right. So we flew to the Edo factory out east. Wiley walked in, met with the owners and the engineers and outlined the problems and suggested some changes in design and installation. After a couple of hours they understood what he was talking about and make the corrections he asked for.

"On the other hand, Wiley could be unpredictable," Doris explained. "One summer, when he was working for Pat Magie, he suddenly was missing. Nobody knew where he had gone. I got a postcard from him saying that he was on Lake Superior at Isle Royale, flying for a company out there. He was on Isle Royale for two months, flew back to Ely and the next day went back to work for Magie just like he had never been gone. Once he flew down to Cloquet for something, kept going south and wound up in Texas where he flew for three weeks."

Doris's folks had a small resort on remote Horse Lake and she flew there every spring when school let out, worked there all summer and never came out until she flew back to town in the fall. With all of that flying going on, she eventually determined it might be a good idea if she took lessons and earned her pilot's license. She told that to Wiley one day as they were flying somewhere, and he simply turned the controls over to her and said: "O.K., fly it."

Doris was determined and began taking regular lessons in Wiley's Aeronca Champ. She progressed through five lessons and was prepared to take the sixth when Wiley informed her he had sold the Champ. Doris said that was as close as she ever came to being a bush pilot.

THE LORELEI

BY BOB CARY

*O*ne summer, the Canadian Customs Officer at Cabin 16 on Basswood Lake brought his attractive young daughter to stay with him, probably to keep an eye on her. This comely young lady, in her late teens, seemed utterly bored with life in a log cabin located in the middle of the wilderness. About all she could find to do was sit out on the rocks in a bathing suit and try to pick up a coat of tan.

One break in the monotony was the occasional arrival of a floatplane checking through the customs station for a trip to some destination in Ontario. The young woman liked to pass time talking with the pilots, particularly a tall, handsome one we shall call Joey. He was young, blonde and dashing, and a strong mutual attraction developed. On several occasions, the young woman asked Joey to take her up for a plane ride and finally, with her father's permission, he did just that. After that, whenever he had some time off, he flew over to the customs station and picked the young lady up. One day, Joey came in with a Cessna 180, picked her up and didn't come back. Not for two months. Her father's anxiety turned to burning anger when word got around the two had flown off to Alaska.

Let it be said this was one of the worst summers U.S. pilots and passengers ever experienced while crossing the border to enter Canada at the Basswood customs station. The irate customs officer, blood in his eye, was reported as ready to shoot Joey if he showed up there again. He took some of his anger out on every seaplane flight coming in, going through every item of luggage, inspecting every piece of cargo, and generally making life miserable for everyone crossing the border.

Eventually, the wayward daughter returned, Joey went to fly

119

elsewhere and life returned pretty well to normal. Joey had the good sense to stay away from the customs station and the good luck to continue with a long and exciting flying career.

U.S. Forest Service crew taking core samples

SAVING *the* GOOD DOCTOR'S PLANE BY JACK HAUTALA

*D*oc Wheeler and his wife were fishing on Ruxton Lake in Canada and when it came time to leave, the snow was so sticky they couldn't take off in their Cessna 180. They decided to put on snowshoes and tramp out a runway. It was dark when they finished, so they got out their camping gear and spent the night in the woods. When morning came, they got ready to take off but found that the wind had switched and the runway they had tramped out was now crosswise to the wind. Doc decided to take off anyway, but as he gathered speed, the plane veered off the packed trail, hit deep snow and flipped over on its nose, which damaged the prop, one ski and one wing.

Doc got on his radio and managed to get a distress call through to an airline operator who relayed the message to Canadian authorities and eventually got the word down to Pat Magie at the Sandy Point base. Magie promptly flew up and rescued Doc and his wife.

Doc Wheeler felt that he could not live without a plane so he promptly bought a Cessna 180 from Magie, using the one sitting on Ruxton Lake for a trade-in. Magie now owned a plane sitting on the ice up in Canada and spring was coming fast. Wiley Hautala and Timmy Thompson flew up to check over the situation and find out what was needed to fly the plane out.

First, they tipped the plane back from its nose in the snow so it was resting on its wheels. Next, they removed the bent propeller, which they flew back to Ely for repairs. A few weeks later Wiley and Jim Kerntz flew back in Kerntz's Cessna 185 but as they tried to land, hit deep slush and were forced to get airborne without stopping. When they circled the area, they noticed a big hole had thawed directly under Doc's airplane and water from the lake surface was draining down the hole. When Wiley returned to Sandy Point, the pilots talked over the situation to decide how to check on the ice thickness at Ruxton Lake. Nobody wanted to land on it to find out.

Mike Tappa was coming up the next weekend in his Super Cub on floats, and I offered to fly up and take a look. Even if the ice broke, the plane on floats wouldn't sink. Obviously, we did not have much, if any, time left before the plane on Ruxton went through the ice and sank.

When Tappa arrived, we flew from Shagawa Lake to Canadian customs at Fort Francis where we landed on water, taxied to the dock and tied up. Al McKenzie, the customs officer, came down to the dock and asked where we were going on floats in winter. We told him we were headed for Ruxton Lake to check the ice under Magie's plane. McKenzie just shook his head and wished us luck.

When we arrived at Ruxton, I thought the best looking ice was on the south part of the lake where we would have plenty of room to take off if the sledding got rough. However, at touchdown, we ran into slush and had a hard time making any headway. Mike said he wanted to take off. As he headed up the lake, we hit the frozen tracks made when Wiley landed in the deep slush earlier. I felt a bump when we hit the ruts and then we accelerated enough to get into the air. Mike said he did not want to try that again and wanted to head home. I argued that we had landed and taken off once and we could do it again. So down we went and landed closer to the airplane where the ice was smooth and would present no trouble in taking off.

We walked over to the Cessna 180 and pushed it away from the hole. The ice thickness measured about 18 inches, enough to hold up the plane. As we walked back to Mike's plane, I saw the right float was tipped underneath at about 30 degrees. A closer look showed that both spreader bars between the floats had bent down and cracked almost through when we hit the ruts. We straightened out the float and used axe handles and a lot of rope to splint the cracked spreader bars, then took off and headed for home.

I kept watching the right float to make sure it didn't fall off. About halfway home, the cracks started to grow and I wished I had used bigger splints. We had to get down and hoped the float wouldn't break clear off and cause a crash. We decided there would be less stress on the damaged spreader bars if we tried landing on water instead of on ice. The only open water was a patch by the tail race at the Winton Power Dam, so we very gently dropped in there. Somewhat relieved, we pulled the plane up on the ice and hiked over to my house, got in my car and drove to see Magie at the seaplane base. We pointed out the situation on Ruxton Lake and said we thought Wiley could probably get in and repair Doc Wheeler's plane before it sank. We also gave Magie the bad news that he now owed Mike Tappa two new spreader bars.

Wiley and Timmy Thompson flew up to Ruxton, put a patch on the back wing spar, cabled the wing to a strut so it wouldn't come loose and put the repaired propeller back on.

It was growing late but Wiley was determined to get the damaged plane back home. He took off and Timmy took off in the other plane. As Timmy gained altitude, he began to look for Wiley but couldn't see him. Timmy was fearful Wiley had crashed. But as he kept looking, he spotted the damaged plane flying just over the treetops. They both made it home ok and saved Magie's plane.

An old Curtiss Robin docked

FLOATPLANE IS SOMETIMES *a* MISNOMER BY JACK HAUTALA

$\mathcal{S}$ome of the hazards of flying floatplanes into granite-rimmed lakes, from northern Minnesota to Hudson Bay, were sharp rocks in the shallows. When going into strange waters, we always circled low over the proposed landing site to look the bottom over very carefully. That is, in those clear lakes where the bottom could be seen. Some of the "dark water" lakes were another problem because rocks just below the surface were difficult to detect. Taxiing to the shore could present problems if there were sunken ledges between the deep water and the shoreline. No matter how careful, every pilot, at one time or another, accidentally banged into rocks. If we were taxiing slowly, the chances were we would bounce off, particularly if the rock had a smooth surface. But if a sharp rock was hit at a good clip, it would rip a hole in the aluminum float.

One result of those hits was that many of the planes, which had been in service for some time, had a patch, or several patches, riveted on one or both floats. And sometimes, after a few more hits, the patches would start to work loose and the float would begin leaking. Trying to take off with a float partially filled with water created another set of problems, particularly if the plane was carrying a heavy load of people and gear.

Floats are equipped with pump-out tubes that allow the water to be pumped out without removing the pontoon covers. Each plane carried a hand pump just for that purpose. However, if the leak was too big and water was coming in too fast, sometimes the only alternative was to run the plane up onto the shore before it sank.

This was the case one day when Kenny Vitek flew one of Pat Magie's Beavers to the Canadian customs and ranger station on

Basswood Lake. He had some fishermen to check through, heading for a destination in Ontario. As Kenny taxied away from the customs dock, he noticed the backs of his floats were under water and sinking deeper. In a cold sweat, he gunned the 450-horse DeHaviland engine and roared across the bay to a point opposite the customs cabin. He intended to run the plane up on the shore, but, unfortunately, the shore at that point was not sloping, but an abrupt dropoff into six feet of water. When the floats hit, the plane stopped. But Kenny was right about one thing—the plane was sinking fast. As the fishermen scrambled out of the cabin and down the floats for shore, the Beaver sank until only the propeller, engine, upper part of the fuselage and the wings were visible. The seaplane base was notified by radio that the plane was sitting on the bottom of Basswood Lake.

Almost immediately, a rescue mission was set in motion. Magie called and asked me to go up and check out the problem. I contacted resort owner Joe Skala who had several outboard boats available. Skala and I took one to Basswood to check the damage. It was sort of a funny sight as we came around the point and saw the wings and part of the fuselage sticking up above the surface. What wasn't funny was the effort it would take to rescue the plane. And the job had to be done before a storm came up and waves took everything.

The plane had gone down on a boulder-strewn bottom, nose against a steep rock bank where there was no way to winch it up on shore without tearing up the floats. The only option seemed to try and lift it out of the lake, drain the floats and run it quickly to some place it could be worked on. We made a list of what we would need in the way of tools and material, took Skala's boat back to the seaplane base and arranged for a work crew to go up in the morning. Magie said he would fly in later in the afternoon with fried chicken for the whole gang.

At daybreak, Joe Skala and I motored up to Basswood with tools, cable, chain and boards, while Magie flew in and dropped off five extra helpers. To hoist the plane out of the lake, we needed a couple of 40-foot poles to make an A-frame. This didn't seem to present any problem since there were hundreds of pine and spruce trees all along the shore. While the Canadian Ranger was irritated about the sunken plane, he was very reluctant to allow any trees cut because it was in a wilderness area. I told him if we didn't get the two trees, there was no way to get the plane out and it would just sit there. Next, he said we would need Canadian work permits in order to work on Canadian soil. But the customs man, who was federal and had more clout, said to hell with it; just get the job done and get the plane out of Canada.

The ranger finally picked out two trees we could use, two skinny ones we didn't feel would do the job; but we had nothing else to work with so we cut the poles, lashed them together for a gin pole to be held in place over the plane at 45 degrees. The frame was anchored by cables clamped to live trees. Boards were nailed across the two poles creating a makeshift ladder.

I climbed out on the A-frame and locked a chain to the peak so it dangled down to the Beaver. From the Forest Service I had borrowed a lifting rig that slid under the fuselage. We connected a coffin hoist from the chain to the lifting rig and started cranking very carefully so the water could drain out of the floats as they came up. The strain on the two trees started our A-frame buckling, so we cut smaller poles for bracing and connected another hoist from the A-frame to a big tree on shore.

After a couple of hours, the Beaver was on top of the water again and floating. A decision was made to fly the empty ship back to the seaplane base where the leaks could be repaired. The Canadian Ranger was extremely happy to see Vitek take off with the Beaver and get out of the park. We pulled down the A-frame and cut the poles into firewood, which was then stacked by the ranger cabin so there was no evidence of what had happened. Skala and I loaded up the cables and equipment in his boat and headed back to Ely.

We had barely left when Magie flew in with a big box of fried chicken for the whole crew. Skala and I were already on the way home, but the extra hands who were helping us that day managed to eat every last wing and drumstick. All Skala and I got was a lot of exercise and a small measure of satisfaction for having figured out how to help an airplane in distress.

One of the Beechcraft 18s that flew out of Wilderness Wings sank in Ontario's Bright Sand Lake. The license number ended in 99-C so that old Beech was nicknamed "99 Charlie." It was a windy day when Pat Magie flew in a bunch of fishermen and when he hit the whitecaps on Bright Sand, the waves tore a patch off the left float. As Magie began to taxi in, he felt the plane getting sluggish and noticed the tail was beginning to settle toward the water. He yelled at the fishermen to crowd forward and at the same time opened the throttle to keep the plane on a level keel. Bright Sand is aptly named and has a number of smooth sand beaches, so it took only moments to ram the Beech up near shore before it sank.

The fishermen, with Stan Levar as guide, took a boat out on the lake to try their luck while Magie radioed for help. Wiley Hautala and Timmy Thompson, the dock boy, flew in with beaching gear and some tools. Beaching gear consists of an aluminum frame with four main wheels that clip onto the sides of the floats and two tail wheels that attach to the back of the floats. Installed while a plane is out on the water, it allows it to be rolled up on shore or onto a ramp.

Pat Magie with 99 Charlie

The fishermen were taken home in the second plane but Levar stayed to help Wiley and Timmy rig the beaching gear. With that in place, 99-C was taxied up on the sand and a temporary patch screwed on to cover the hole. It was in a particularly bad spot on the step where most of the stress occurs during landings and take-offs. With the patch in place, they rolled the airplane back into the lake, removed the beaching wheels, loaded up everything and prepared to take off. Wiley had the Beech almost up to flying speed when the new patch tore off and the plane slowed down as water poured into the hole. Instead of getting off the water, they taxied back to the beach and reinstalled the beaching gear. Then they decided to move the plane to a better spot, started the two engines and began to taxi down the bay. At this point one wheel on the beaching gear hit a boulder and stopped operating. This caused the plane to begin going in crazy circles. In short order, the damaged float filled with water and the plane sank with the left float, left wing and the tail in the lake. The good right float and the damaged beaching gear kept the plane fairly upright.

Of course, back at Sandy Point, we did not know of the additional problem and we sat around waiting for Wiley to fly in with the Beech. At about 6 p.m., Magie was pacing the floor and asked if I would fly up to Bright Sand in Jim Kerntz's Cessna 172 and check out the problem. Kerntz decided to fly along, too, so we took off for Bright Sand. The weather was clear and as we came over the lake we could see the Twin Beech out in the water with the tail and left wing submerged. Wiley, Stan Levar and Timmy were standing on the shore.

After we taxied up, we held a discussion concerning the problem, made out a list of necessary tools and then took off for Ely with Levar on board. Wiley and Timmy offered to stay on the shore all night and be ready to go in the morning when the work crew arrived.

It was 9 p.m. before we got going and it was pitch black as we flew over the wilderness toward home. At 10:30 we saw the lights of Ely, swung over Winton, heading west toward Shagawa Lake. I touched down OK and taxied to the Seaplane dock at Sandy Point where Magie helped us tie up. He quickly grasped the situation, got on the phone and called some friends in Duluth and Virginia, lining up four more planes, ten people and a lot of tools including an air compressor, power drills, bags of Styrofoam balls, a coffin hoist and coils of rope.

At daybreak, I flew Kerntz's C-172 to Bright Sand to find the other four planes were already there. First, we placed big truck inner tubes under the sunken float and the sunken wing and inflated them to try and get the craft up high enough to pump out the float, but it didn't work. Finally, we had a scuba diver attach a rope to the sunken float's beaching gear and ran it to a hoist on shore. Winching was slow work because the hoist had only 15 feet of cable and we had to reconnect it every 15 feet. The diver swam ahead of the plane, removing any rocks that were in the way as we slowly cranked 99 Charlie to shore. By afternoon we had the plane up shallow enough so the sunken pontoon was partially afloat and we started pumping it out. The power unit fizzled, so we took turns pumping by hand. It took an hour to remove 1,000 gallons of water, but finally the plane was floating and Wiley taxied it to the beach where we could work on it.

All the additional crew loaded up their gear and took off in the four planes leaving Wiley, Timmy and me to finish the job. This time we jammed the compartment full of Styrofoam balls and bolted the patch to the float because we didn't want the plane to sink again. We worked until dark, then slept in the cabin of the Beech. At daybreak, we finished the work and loaded up all the gear. Then Timmy and I waded alongside the floats removing the beaching gear as Wiley taxied slowly toward deeper water. The detached beaching gear was being stowed through the side door as fast as Timmy and I could move. Wiley, worried that the damaged float might again take on water, was watching intently from the cockpit window and as soon as he saw the last piece of beaching gear go into the plane, he gunned the twin engines to start his takeoff run. I was still standing on the left float by the side door and when he went to full power, I was blown off the float into the lake. I swam until my feet hit bottom and then waded over to Kerntz's C-172, climbed in soaking wet and headed for home.

Wiley flew right over Ely, not wishing to risk another landing and takeoff, and put down at the lake near Eveleth where the float could be properly repaired at Bill Martilla's lakeside metal shop. I drove to Eveleth and since I was the only one with riveting experience and small enough to slide inside the float compartment, that's where I spent the next four days. The heat inside the float was terrible, like a microwave, and I kept drinking ice cold beer to stay alive. I took off four days without pay from my regular job at the power plant to get 99 Charlie back up and running. You might say I loved that old twin engine workhorse.

BUSH PILOTS & "WILD" LIFE

*"One thing I knew from
that day on in Alaska is that we
humans are definitely not at the
top of the food chain."*

WHEN LAKE TROUT ARE RUNNING

BY BOB CARY

*T*he ice was off the smaller lakes and just breaking up on the larger ones that April day when Kenny Bellows and I decided to go to Canada for lake trout. The customs officer was at Sand Point Lake and Mike O'Brien, the Ontario Parks Ranger was at the Lac La Croix cabin a five minute hop away. We loaded up Kenny's 180 Cessna with a 3-horse outboard motor, gas, fishing tackle, lashed a 15-foot Grumman square stern canoe to the left float and headed north.

It was a warm day for April, overcast but fairly quiet. As we came in over La Croix, we could see huge cakes of ice floating free on the lake but the area next to the ranger's cabin was clear. Kenny laid the aircraft down smoothly, and we taxied up to the dock.

Mike O'Brien came running down the dock, a 12-foot boat hook in hand, to greet his first visitors of the season. As we taxied up and cut power, Mike caught the front cleat on the left float with the steel boat hook, pulled us in close and Kenny swung down to grab a tie rope.

At that point, the ranger placed the point of the pole in the middle of Kenny's back and with a great shove, sent him flailing into the icy lake. I ran to help pull Kenny out, who was gasping and coughing water, then we both turned on O'Brien.

It had been a lonely few days waiting for someone to show up at the ranger station and apparently Mike had brought in several quarts of Canadian rye along with his other supplies. He stood there, rocking back and forth on his heels, his Irish laughter echoing from the woods. "Were ye ready fer an early spring dip, eh?" he roared.

"You're drunk!" Kenny sputtered.

"No, not totally, but I've had a wee nip," Mike shot back.

"Come on up to the cabin. I've got a hot fire and I'll dry you off."

In a half hour Kenny was thawed and dried out. We hopped in the canoe and headed for Rebecca Falls where we nailed a half dozen fat lake trout in the churning current below the cataract. Then we motored back to the ranger cabin, enjoyed a hot cup of coffee with Mike, loaded up our gear and fish. Kenny kept a sharp eye on Mike as he lashed the canoe to the float, but nothing more occurred.

When we were in the air, Kenny remarked: "Can you believe Mike would knock me into the lake like that?"

"It could have been worse," I said.

"How?" Kenny asked, trimming the flaps.

"It could have been me instead of you," I replied.

COUNTING *the* DEAD

$\mathcal{K}$enny Bellows had several thousand hours flying on floats before he migrated from Minnesota to Alaska seeking work. His credentials were excellent, and when he went looking for a flying job he immediately picked up a contract flying a wildlife research team from the Alaska Game and Fish Commission on a blacktail deer survey.

Every fall, blacktail deer migrate from their high country summer range down to the coast where food is easier to find. At the end of winter, the deer migrate back into the mountains, all except for the ones that don't make it through to spring. By counting the remains of dead deer along segments of the coast each spring, researchers can get a good estimate of how the population is doing—at least what the trend is in the herd.

Thus it was, on an early spring day, Kenny flew a pair of researchers to a large bay on the coast south of Sitka to conduct a study. As they circled over the bay, the researchers pointed out where they wanted to be dropped off and where Kenny could meet them later on a grassy point a half mile up the coast. They intended to hike the shoreline counting deer carcasses on their way back to the plane a mile away. When he was dropping them off, one of the game and fish men looked Ken over carefully. "You got a gun in the plane?" he inquired.

"No, what would I need a gun for?" Ken asked.

"Bears. There are a lot of grizzlies along the coast right now feeding on the dead deer."

Being from Minnesota, Ken didn't bat an eye. "I've been around bears all my life and never felt the need to carry a gun."

And this was true. However, Kenny's experience was with black bears. Alaskan grizzlies are not only a whole lot larger but have a somewhat different outlook on the world.

In any event, the game and fish people got off on shore and Kenny taxied across the bay to a grassy point where he would meet them later. He hit shore, climbed down from the cabin, stepped out on the bank and proceeded to turn the plane around, facing it toward the sea. Gripping the tail section, he tugged the floats inshore so the rudders rested securely on the gravel; then he sat down to wait. "It was a warm, sunshiny spring day," Kenny recalls, "and the grassy point was level and smooth. I stretched out and took a nap. I have no idea how long I slept but I awoke to somebody yelling. Down the shore a couple of hundred yards were the game and fish guys waving their arms and yelling something at me."

Kenny Bellows

Kenny sat up, puzzled, wondering why they didn't just finish hiking that short distance up the coastline. "I stood up," he remembered, "and heard a low growl. Looking around I was startled to see a huge grizzly a few yards away closing in fast, eyes glittering, jaws wide open. In a split second I realized that the researchers had spotted the big bear stalking me and were trying to get my attention and warn me."

Now on his feet, Kenny sprinted for the plane. "That bear was almost on me as I leaped on the left float, yanked the cockpit door open and flipped the ignition key, all in one motion."

135

The prop turned over, the engine coughed a cloud of white exhaust and Kenny hit the throttle with the bear one step away from the floats. As he taxied over to pick up the two wildlife researchers, he got a good look at a very large and angry grizzly standing on the grassy point, frustrated by being cheated out of a bush pilot he was going to have for lunch.

"Last time I ever flew anywhere in Alaska without a gun," Kenny concluded. "Alaskan grizzlies are big. And they can be mean and very unpredictable. Most of the time they mind their own business, but when one takes a notion to hunt you, you had better be ready." Twice, in his later years in Alaska, Kenny was called upon to fly in where an individual had an unfortunate encounter with a bear. Once Kenny flew out a man's rib cage in a bag and once he flew out a man's boot with the foot still in it.

"Bears don't usually have a whole lot of leftovers when they have you for dinner," is Kenny's matter-of-fact comment.

When talk involves Alaskan grizzlies, Kenny sometimes refers to one he met under some unusual circumstances on a hunting trip with his son Lance.

"A friend of mine had a .357 Weatherby rifle in mint condition with a fine checkered stock and was willing to part with it because he was short of cash. My son Lance and I were planning an elk hunt, and I was sure the Weatherby had a good whallop and would fill the bill admirably. I forked over the money and took the rifle home. I was busy with some flying and didn't get a chance to look over the new gun before we packed up and left. Never got a chance to sight it in, but the previous owner assured me that he had hunted with it often and it was 'right on the money.' Anyway, I was not particularly fired up about shooting an elk; I just hoped that Lance would get a chance at a nice bull.

"We flew the floatplane to the elk hunting area, set up camp and began to scout out the terrain. It was a swampy area, lots of lowland brush with relatively poor visibility. We split up and worked our way through the brush, reading sign, noting hoof prints, but not spotting any elk.

"Frustrated with the lack of visibility in the lowland, I worked my way toward a knoll covered with rocks and scrub—one that might afford a good view of the surrounding area—a place from which I might spot a set of antlers.

"After some effort I got to the knoll and began climbing

toward the top. Just as I was about to reach the crest, I came face to face with an enormous grizzly. Not only big, but obviously angry. He reared up on his back legs, growled, clicked his teeth, rolled his head from side to side and appeared about ready to charge.

"It was a tight situation. He was about 15 paces away as I swung up the .357 and steadied the sights between his eyes. We stared at each other for a moment, the bear growling ferociously and me hoping I would not have to shoot. First, I did not want the bear and, second, he was uphill from me and even a brain shot would send him rolling down directly on top of me, which could be bad for both of us.

In Alaska, pilots carry sawed-off 12-gauge shotguns with slugs

"Very carefully, keeping the gun sight steady on his head, I took a half step backward. He growled but didn't move. Then I took another step. And another. Slowly, I edged back down the knoll, the bear still growling but not following me. I hit the brushy flat and moved away quickly but carefully, listening to make sure I wasn't being followed.

"Back at camp I related my adventure to Lance and we both had a good laugh over it. 'Can I take a look at your new gun?' Lance asked. I slipped it out of the case and handed it over. Lance studied its fine finish and sleek design. 'How's it shoot?' he asked.

"Never got to fire it," I said. "I bought it just before the trip and never had a chance to sight it in.

"Care if I put a few rounds through it?" Lance asked.

"I nodded in agreement and he stuffed a few shells in his pocket and went to the edge of the woods. I waited for a shot but didn't hear any. A couple of minutes later Lance returned. He solemnly handed the gun back and looked me in the eye. 'The gun won't fire,' he said. 'The action is broken.'

"Cold, sweaty fingers of fear crawled up my neck into my scalp. I suddenly realized I had stared down a huge grizzly with an absolutely useless rifle. Fortunately, the griz didn't want my hide any more than I wanted his. Lance and I figured we didn't care to hunt with that bear hanging around so we loaded up the plane and flew to another location.

"Two things I learned about traveling in Alaskan bear country: It pays to carry a gun, and it pays to make sure that gun is ready to shoot."

GRIZZLIES *and* ICE WATER BY BOB CARY

*T*om Dayton, who is currently flying out of Sitka, Alaska, observes that most floatplane pilots have gotten their feet and knees wet more than once and a few may have experienced the surprise of full immersion. Tom is one who went in over his head—way over—in cold salt water soon after he first came to Alaska as a bush pilot in the Juneau area.

The company, for which Tom began flying, sent him with an veteran bush pilot in order for him to become familiar with the areas he would normally be servicing—logging camps, fishing villages and native settlements, some in the middle of nowhere. On this day, they were flying a seven-passenger Beaver on a 20-minute flight south of Juneau to pick up a group of tourists. With passengers aboard, the veteran pilot would do the flying. When they were empty, Tom was at the controls.

"We were to pick up tourists who had spent the morning doing what many Alaskans consider an insane activity—getting close to grizzly bears."

For a fee, plus airfare out and back, wide-eyed tourists, kids and grandparents would spend several hours in the wilderness on a small peninsula north of Admiralty Island, getting within 30 feet of several grizzly bears that frequent the area. The brochure advertises great picture-taking opportunities with lunch included, but it doesn't say what's on the menu or who is going to eat it. In all fairness to the people who run the tour, it should be said that these particular bears had gotten used to human presence through years of associating with a trapper and fisherman who once lived there. This independent soul finally died and left a legacy of mild-mannered bruins. As long as they received the food they'd gotten used to, they'd tolerate the presence of upright, two-legged critters. So both species got lunch and nobody got hurt. But it seemed like a tenuous agreement at best and perhaps not really understood that well by the bears.

"It may be that I'm overly cautious and skeptical about bears, but I've heard that they're unpredictable as sharks and not at all picky about what they eat. Perhaps my attitude is a direct result of being shown, on the day my wife and I arrived in Alaska, pictures of the latest griz attack."

The photos showed the skeletal remains of a man, everything eaten except his two feet encased in boots. The boots were apparently too much trouble for the bear to remove. "One thing I knew from that day on in Alaska," Tom said, "is that we humans are definitely not at the top of the food chain."

It was with these thoughts in mind that he flew over the peninsula where this 'natural' activity was taking place. He could see the people standing in a group with bears on three sides, some only 15 feet away. "Crazy," Tom thought to himself as he studied the bay for wind direction and submerged rocks.

Tom Dayton

Tom circled and landed. Small ripples on the water allowed a smooth landing and a fast taxi toward shore. Slowing down, he noted there were several ropes in the water anchoring a small floathouse in place. These shelters, like mobile homes, are set up on log rafts and are common on coastal Alaskan waters.

"To get over the ropes is usually a simple maneuver—just run over them and lift the pontoon rudders as the line passes below. The first rope went just like that, but the second one somehow caught the float and stopped our progress. I pushed on the rudder, thinking that a different angle might allow the rope to release, but no luck, so I shut down the engine and got out to investigate."

The rope was about ¾ inches in diameter and had caught where the aluminum keel turned upward at 90 degrees. "I thought it would be no problem to push the rope down with a paddle, using the one we had lashed to the struts. I pushed the rope downward and well below the bottom of the float, but without results. I tried several more times at various angles and kneeled on the float to push the paddle deeper. No luck."

On the beach, fifty yards away, the tourists were watching with interest and perhaps beginning to sense their situation. They had already said their goodbyes to the bears. They'd probably taken more photos than was polite and the bears were getting restless. It had been some time since lunch, and they were beginning to feel like dinner. And the taxi was stuck in the bay.

"I consulted with the other pilot for suggestions. He had none. After all, he didn't get the plane stuck. It was becoming painfully obvious that I was not going to get the aircraft to the shore without getting wet." Tom's reluctance to accept this plan of action sooner was based not only on a lack of proper swimming attire, but also on the latitude. Early summer water surface temperature in southeast Alaska may read 50 degrees, but feels like 35, which is why there is not a lot of swimming in the ocean there.

"The bears were now getting more restless and the tourists were getting more nervous while me and the plane were getting nowhere. Nothing to do but pull off my boots, strip to my underwear and dive down off the float into the ice water. One quick tug on the rope from underneath and we were free. I scrambled out of the water, onto the float, wrung out my soaked underwear, dried off with my shirt, pulled on my pants and taxied to the shore.

"The people said they enjoyed taking photos of the show. The bears, in the meantime, had gotten bored with the whole deal and meandered off. My baptism in the ice water had me wide awake and assured my membership in the Alaskan Pilots' Polar Bear Club."

All in a day's work for a floatplane jockey.

HE WANTED *to* FISH *and* HUNT

*F*rom the time he was old enough to stick a worm on a hook, one of Dan Houle's two major aims in life was to catch fish. The other one emerged when he was a few years older: Go hunting.

By the time he was 25 years old, he owned a bait and tackle store in Forest Lake, Minnesota. But this was not enough. From reading outdoor magazines, he determined that the most exciting fishing and hunting had to be in Alaska and the only way to experience it was by becoming a floatplane pilot.

"I had a vision in my mind—I wanted to fly a DeHaviland Beaver in the Alaskan bush," Houle recalled.

Acting on his goal, he visited nearby Crystal Flyway to take lessons, paying for some of them by pumping gas and doing odd jobs around the field.

"There were a number of young men taking flying lessons, but I was the only one who insisted he was going to be a bush pilot."

From there he enrolled in the Minneapolis Vocational Technical School where he earned a license for aircraft maintenance, figuring mechanical skills might get him closer to Alaska.

Next, he picked up his floatplane rating in a J-3 Cub at a flying school in Hayward, Wisconsin, then headed for northern Minnesota, at that time a mecca for bush pilots. Flight operations at Bohman Airways, International Falls, was looking for a mechanic and hired Houle. While servicing Bohman's aircraft, he flew occasionally with pilots in Beavers and absorbed bush pilot lore from old-timers on the Bohman staff. One winter day the company had a Beaver on skis that conked out on an ice fishing trip to Ontario's Pekagoning Lake. The anglers were flown out in another aircraft and Houle was flown in with tools, food and a sleeping bag to find the problem with the engine and fix it, no matter how long it took.

"I began tearing the engine down in bitter cold," Houle noted. "Overnight I slept in the plane's cabin to keep out of the wind."

He eventually determined the problem was with the valves, which he set about cleaning and re-seating. Lacking proper gauging tools, he used the cover of a match book for a gauge. "It looked about the right thickness and it turned out I was right.

"In the morning, I put everything back together, locked down the cowl and started up the engine. It kicked right off like new. The plan had been for me to camp out by the plane, call in on the radio when I had the engine running and wait until a pilot came in to fly the Beaver out, but I figured it was my project, so I took off from Pekagoning and headed back. I had a few dual hours in the Beaver so I wasn't much concerned."

As he approached International Falls, Houle called in on the radio: "Beaver 897 coming in!"

The startled radio operator asked who was flying the plane. When Houle identified himself there was a silence and then the operator came back in a somewhat strangled voice, acknowledging his approach and ordering caution.

Houle landed the Beaver flawlessly and reported to the office. The operations manager looked the youngster over coolly and said: "I guess that was your check flight. And I guess you go to work flying full time tomorrow."

"In one instant I was a bush pilot. My next goal was to fly in Alaska, but I had more hours to pile up and also needed to earn a living, no matter how much I wanted to join the ducks and geese migrating north."

In the meantime, romance entered Dan's life in the form of Lori, a girl who shared a strong interest in the outdoors. When fall came, they were married and flew to Ontario's Turtle River on a "hunting moon." Both scored on big bulls. It was about then they started making plans for Alaska. Dan continued flying for Bohman, piling up hours on the Beaver.

It was a year before they finally packed up and headed for King Salmon, Alaska, where Dan had hired on to fly the bush. In the meantime they had become parents, but undeterred, they headed north with their guns, fishing tackle, the baby and $100 cash.

Dan flew 12 seasons in Alaska, six of them at King Salmon. Among the celebrities he flew in for salmon fishing were TV newscaster Dan Rather and noted test pilot and Air Force veteran Chuck Yeager. "Most of the VIPs we flew in were nothing like they were portrayed in the press. Maybe it was because they were on vacation and fishing, but they were all great people, just a lot of fun to be with," Dan notes. "And they understood aircraft. Rather said he had been forced down a couple of times covering the combat in Vietnam. I flew several trips with Yeager. He always requested that I fly him in, saying that I knew where to find the fish."

One year he flew for Mark Air Express out of Kuskowin, flying entirely to remote native villages. "I flew a Cessna Caravan, a turbo prop, Cessna 207 and some others, all on ice and in terrific winds. After a while, I got to appreciate the winds. When we were hauling extra heavy loads, they helped get the planes into the air."

As an illustration of some unique cargo loads, he noted that once he flew 1500 pounds of shotgun shells in the Cessna Caravan to a settlement on the Kuskowin River. "When I landed, the Upik village spokesman called all the people together and announced: "Hey! Dan just flew in with a cargo of emergency supplies. He just came in with the shotgun shells we need for the spring goose hunt!"

Lori Houle and family

Not all the Alaskan memories are good ones. His friend Ernest Gallo was scheduled to fly in and pick up passengers on a terribly windy day. "I told Ernie he shouldn't be going on this flight," Houle said, "that he shouldn't try it. But Ernie was afraid of nothing. He went anyway. I saw his plane go in," Houle said. "Three of them on board. It was terrible."

Dan and Lori Houle

One element pilots all mention concerning Alaskan flying is the prevalence of grizzly bears. Houle's friend Steve Bergeron had a sportsman who won an Alaskan bear hunting trip at a Ducks Unlimited dinner. He flew in the hunter, set up camp, cooked supper and turned in. They noticed that a bear had visited the campsite earlier and caused considerable damage, but they figured that one was long gone elsewhere. Not so. They woke up in the middle of the night with the bear stamping around inside the tent. Steve grabbed his rifle, but in the dark could not see the bear so he swung the gun muzzle around until it connected with fur and he pulled the trigger. In addition to the deafening sound of the shot inside the tent, there was a horrendous roar and a ripping sound as the wounded grizzly went crashing out. Steve found a flashlight, stepped out with his rifle and finished off the big invader.

The wholly terrified hunter wanted to quit right there. He said he'd had enough of Alaskan bears, particularly those that came inside tents. But Steve, not wishing to lose a guide fee, got the hunter settled down and convinced him they would do OK from that point on. Somewhat reluctantly, the hunter agreed and they went out to scout the surrounding country. As luck would have it, they came upon a huge grizzly. Steve whispered to the hunter to shoot, but the hunter was either overexcited or frightened. Instead of anchoring the big bruin, he merely wounded it. The roaring bear rolled around on the ground, tearing up brush and gravel, then started toward his tormentors.

"Shoot! Shoot again!" Steve yelled, keeping his eyes on the rapidly approaching bear. The shot never came. Steve glanced around and was startled to see his hunter 200 yards away leaving the scene at a fast sprint. With the bear almost on him, Steve whirled around and nailed the grizzly, ending the episode.

After twelve seasons in Alaska, Houle and his family returned to the lower 48 states, migrating to northern Minnesota where he taught aviation at the Community College in Ely, managed the local airport and set up a small fly-in service of his own. Lori, a skilled dog musher, acquired a dog team and began operating winter trips into the nearby wilderness. Politics knocked Houle out of the airport job and the flying business failed to prosper. At the time of this writing, Dan was involved in real estate, was doing some guiding and preparing to take over the operation of a small Canadian resort across the lake and east of Kettle Falls on big Rainy Lake. He intends to operate a single plane for his own use but has no plans for any large commercial flying.

Alaska? He's been there and done that, but he may not be finished up there, either. He's keeping his options open.

Dan Houle

THE KIDNEY PROBLEM

BY BOB CARY

*W*hen Tom Dayton quit flying jet fighters for the Navy at the end of the Vietnam War, he knew he wanted to keep flying. He had been a wilderness canoe guide during his college years and set his sights on floatplanes. His first move was to get checked out on pontoons in northern Minnesota, then headed for Alaska where he flew for Bellair at Sitka.

"In the native Klingit language," Tom explains, "Sitka is a word meaning 'strewn about' like a farmer throwing corn to his chickens. This is how it looks; islands are all over the large bay off the west coast of Baranof Island. It is where Sitka is located and an area we fly to a lot."

An unforgettable trip for Tom was a mission in a Cessna 185 to pick up two young women at Baranof Warm Springs harbor on the opposite side of the island, a small settlement popular with tourists and fishermen because of the hot sulfur springs where a person can soak and relax. In addition, he had a man to pick up some distance away at a Rowan Bay logging camp.

"It was one of those clear blue days when I took off," Tom recalled. "A flight that would normally take about 45 minutes."

He had a 15-minute climb up the steep mountain valley east of Sitka, cut through a saddle-type pass at 3500 feet and dropped into the long, green valley where a thundering, frothy waterfall marked the approach to Warm Springs on the east side of Baranof Island.

Tom circled and touched down close to the dock to minimize taxi time. The two young ladies climbed in the back and Tom took off for Rowan Bay.

When they saw he was not heading back over the mountain pass to Sitka, they asked why they were heading east over the water. Tom explained to them about the third passenger, and a longer flight.

"If we had known it was going to be this long, we would have used the bathroom before we left," one complained.

"Sorry about that, but it won't be much longer," he promised, aiming the Cessna at the distant mountains that defined the most direct route to Rowan Bay. "My passenger was waiting at the dock with his satchel. He loaded in and we were off immediately. I gave the standard radio call to our dispatcher:

"Bellair Four-Eight Quebec, off Rowan for Sitka with three."

"Roger that," said Dee Bellows, dispatcher at the Sitka float-plane base. "The weather is starting to roll here, so you might not be able to get over the top."

"OK," Tom said, "I'll plan on Whale Bay–Gut Bay Pass." This would lengthen the flight time even more, but was a lot safer.

Clouds were quietly hovering in the mountains of eastern Baranof Island as he flew through the pass at a comfortable 2500 feet. On the other side, however, the Pacific coastal situation was a totally different story. The weather was terrible and conditions grew steadily worse as the plane flew northwest in a driving gale hammering the wave-battered coast. Ordinarily, this would have been magnificent scenery. The rugged shore was interspersed with deep bays, forested highlands, patches of tundra and dozens of foamy cascades. Now, it was fairly well obscured.

"The closer we got to Sitka, the more I could see that fog had filled the whole bay. I called the Flight Service Station at Sitka. In my headset I heard: 'Four-Eight Quebec! Sitka is below the minimum. A special VFR is required to enter the Sitka Control Zone! State your intentions.'"

From the back seat came a plaintive cry: "We have to pee!"

"For a moment I considered landing at a beach to relieve them, but, after all, these were tough Alaskan women who are known to roll their own cigarettes, get mud on their rubber boots, chew tobacco and get very upset if you pick up their chainsaw. I decided not to waste fuel on another takeoff and just keep flying."

Tom got a clearance from Flight Service at Sitka but was assigned number four, in line behind three other aircraft arriving from different directions. "The fog bank just the other side of Baranof Point looked ominous, so I decided to use my waiting time to look for an alternative route."

"We've got to pee!" came the squawk from the back. Tom nodded and kept flying, heading southeast to Deep Bay, looking for a back door, but this was shut down just ten miles short of Sitka.

"Why aren't we there yet? Why are we flying circles?" screeched the women. "We have to go NOW!"

"I tried to explain about the Zone and the delay, then called Bellair to let them know why I was taking so long to return.

"Base owner Ken Bellows came on the phone to explain: 'It's clear back here! Maybe you should try the back door through Deep Bay.'"

A pair of ladies on a fishing trip in Alaska

"Uh-huh. Been there. Done that," Tom answered. He circled just outside the Control Zone, awaiting his turn for the Special VFR Clearance. "Not only was there a back seat bladder crisis, but I was now afflicted with an attack of 'get home-itis' caused by fuel depletion." When clearance came, he headed straight into the fog about 30 feet above the waves. There was an instant change in visibility, like flying into a dense bunch of wispy curtains. He followed the shoreline for reference, which was all he could see, staying just above the waves. There was more chatter on the radio, but his attention was focused on flying and navigating. Visibility worsened and Tom lowered the flaps on the 185, intently seeking that 'clear back here' that Kenny had announced.

"This was not a good place to be with perhaps 400 yards of

visibility, and I stared into the fog, apprehensive that a cruise ship might be laying along the coast and we would suddenly wind up plastered on the superstructure. At that point there was a thunderous 'WHAM!' as we dropped too low and the floats hit the top of that 'ninth big wave.' It was then that I looked down to see the rudder pedals shaking. Next, I realized it was my feet that were causing this strange effect. Funny, I thought, how one's nervous system reacts to a mixture of adrenaline and fear. It was time to set down and stop before we all became a headline in next day's Sitka Daily Sentinel.

"I banked into the fog-shrouded cove and landed the plane where the waves were only running four feet high. While riding this, I checked the map to try and find my exact position. Luckily the front seat passenger was a fisherman who had boated along this stretch and helped recognize shoreline landmarks."

At this point, the airport called saying: "Four-Eight Quebec! What's your position?"

"Sitka! Four-Eight Quebec is on the water in Baranof Cove."

The controller came back: "Five-One Delta, what is your position?"

Five-One Delta came on: "Sitka, I am on the water right behind Four-Eight Quebec."

Tom jerked his head around and looked back in surprise. Bobbing on the waves directly behind him was Five-One Delta. Then he understood what that radio chatter had been all about earlier. They had recognized his Bellair insignia and followed close on his tail, believing he knew exactly were he was going.

"Whatta we do now?" came the desperate cry from the back seat.

"Without saying anything I taxied in the general direction of Sitka, riding the waves, keeping some of the island in view and hoping for enough visibility to eventually take off." The waves diminished gradually as he got farther into the Sound. Finally, he taxied behind an island and found a little better visibility, turned into the wind, raised the water rudders and gave the 185 full throttle. In a few moments he broke out of the fog and into the 'clear back here' Kenny had promised. "I called Sitka Flight Service, found my clearance was now number three behind an Alaska Airlines jet and Five-One Delta, of all people, who had recently been following me and was now cleared ahead of me."

Since it would now take another five minutes or more of circling to come in, Tom turned to the ladies in back to explain what was going on. "You'd better land this plane right now or you're going to have a mess in the back seat," one lady yelled.

"Lady!" he yelled back. "After what we just flew through, that wouldn't be anything compared to the mess we could have had up here in the front seat!

"I never did hear any more from Five-One Delta. Oh, and the women made it to the toilet. Just barely."

NEVER TOO COLD

*"Not many people can understand
how desperate you can get
out in the woods all alone in the
winter when you run out of cigars."*

ESCAPE SHACK

BY JACK HAUTALA

$\mathcal{B}$ack before the Boundary Waters became a wilderness by government decree, there were a lot of people living out there. There had been a couple of Native American settlements, some forty resorts and a lot of private cabins. And some shacks. The shacks and cabins largely belonged to local men who liked to hunt, fish and trap or had problems with their wives and used the shacks for escape.

Runjack "Runny" Mackie was one of the men who simply had a great love for the woods. When city life became a burden, he simply loaded up a couple of packsacks and headed for his cabin on remote Fourtown Lake. One summer Runny went up there, stayed through the hunting season and then didn't come out. There was not a lot of concern because Runny was pretty self-sufficient, but his friends wondered a little.

When the first freeze came on Shagawa Lake, I put my little two-seat J-3 Cub on skis and invited Jim Kobe to go for a ride. Inevitably, we flew north over Fourtown Lake and dropped down for a look at Runny's domain. At this point, Runny came out of the shack waving his arms frantically.

"Runny's in some kind of trouble," Kobe noted. "We ought to go down and check him out."

The only thing was, I didn't know how much ice we had on Fourtown Lake and if it would hold the plane. Kobe and I talked it over and decided to test the ice. I flew down, hit the surface and taxied fast over the snow and ice while Jim climbed out the right hand door, got on the right ski and then jumped off into the snow. As he went rolling over and over, I gunned the engine and went back up in the sky.

Kobe had my hand axe from the plane, cut a hole and signaled the ice was thick enough to hold me. I went down, taxied over to where he and Runny Mackie were standing and shut off the power. When I climbed out of the cab, I noticed Mackie seemed OK, but I asked, "What kind of trouble are you in?"

"I ran out of cigars," Runny replied.

While Kobe and I nearly fell on the ice laughing, Runny seriously explained that he needed a ride to town to get some cigars and pleaded for us to give him a lift. I stopped laughing long enough to agree but said that since we had only a two-seater, I would fly Jim to town and then come back. On the return, Runny apologized for the inconvenience and explained that he had intended to come out earlier but a quick freeze caught him at the shack. Then the weather turned warm for a few days, and he was afraid the ice wouldn't hold if he started to walk out.

When I dropped Runny and his old Duluth pack off at Ely, he thanked me profusely for my concern over my well being, noting, "Not many people can understand how desperate you can get out in the woods all alone in the winter when you run out of cigars."

He was probably right.

Reeling in a salmon in Alaska's ice and fog

A WHOLE LOTTA BULL BY BOB CARY

"*H*ey! Hey! Everybody up! Time to get rolling, eh?"

The shout was emphasized by a fist banging on the bedroom door. It was 4 a.m. and totally dark outside, even with a thick layer of snow on the ground.

My wife mumbled something unpleasant as I climbed out of bed, padded across the cold floor in my bare feet and jerked the door open. Standing in the hall in his shorts and holding a wet bottle of Molson beer in his left hand was bush pilot Earl Thurier.

"Hey! The moose will be moving. Time to get breakfast and in the air."

It was obvious Earl was drinking his breakfast. Quite a feat after partying half the night in some of Atikokan's livelier watering holes. Owner of Crystal Lake Lodge and Airways, Earl was about as wild a woods character as one might chose to find. Or, perhaps, not choose to find. But he was a skilled bush pilot and one heck of a moose hunter. It was the latter ability that brought my wife, my daughter Barb and me to this remote part of Ontario in midwinter. Two years previous, Barb and I had hunted with Earl and fellow pilot Eddie Kaluza at Eddie's Island Camp on Sandford Lake. On that expedition, Barb had dropped an 1,100-pound bull, not bad for a 16-year-old high schooler. That moose kept the family in meat for a year. This was another meat safari.

At the kitchen table, Earl's wife served up smoking plates of scrambled eggs and sausage while the pilot and his son Gerald studied a large scale map of the hunting area. "There's a half dozen moose hanging out up here," Earl poked the map with his forefinger. "No place to get the plane in there. You'll have to go in on snowmobiles, and I'll land on this lake a mile away. If you knock one down, I'll hear the shots and buzz over to see how it looks."

Gerald and Earl Thurier loading moose quarters

By five we were chewing through ruts on snowpacked back-roads in Gerald's pickup truck. The headlights glinted on drifts piled high as the cab windows, typical for late December. An hour and a half brought us to the road's end, terminus of several snowed-over logging trails. We climbed down and by flashlight unloaded two Ski-Doos, lashed on our rifle cases, stowed thermos and lunch in a packsack and started over the snow. Like a timberwolf in home territory, Gerald guided the lead machine up hill and down, through tall spruce and patches of cutover, mile after mile. Barb and I followed, doubling up on the second machine. It was sunup when he pulled into a small clearing, circled and cut the power. After the drone of the snowmobiles, the silence was almost loud.

With his mitten, Gerald indicated three sets of moose tracks crossing the clearing and filing down a logging trail. "From here we go on snowshoe," he whispered. "They probably didn't travel far in this deep snow...we'll see. Oh, and from now on we don't talk."

With Gerald breaking trail, we plodded through the soft fluff, the only sound the soft swoosh of our snowshoe webs. About a mile from the machines, the trail forked around a triangle patch of dark spruce. Gerald studied the tracks, motioned for me to skirt the woods on the right while he would circle left. He indicated that Barb should stay where she was on the tracks in case the animals doubled back on their trail.

Where the three moose entered the spruce, their tracks veered right, parallel to my path. It had begun to snow again, reducing visibility but also creating excellent conditions for a stalk. A slight movement ahead caught my eye and I stopped. Eventually, I made out the head of a moose lying down, flicking its big ears to shake off the flakes. Edging ahead, I was about to raise the rifle when a bull crashed out of a thicket next to me and a third moose jumped up farther ahead. I cracked off a shot at the disappearing bull, heard him grunt and saw his head droop, but he recovered and kept going, all three moose lumbering away in the heavy snow. Subsequently, they ran into Gerald at the far end of the spruce patch. His rifle cracked four times and then the forest went silent as I hurried ahead.

Earl Thurier at White Otter Lake

Gerald was sitting on the bull contemplating the carnage. All three moose were dead; the bull I hit had dropped just as it came into his view. He nailed one cow face-on and the other cow as it broke to his left.

"Boy, we've got the year's meat for both our families," I exulted.

Gerald looked worried. "We've got a big job ahead. We're almost two miles from the nearest lake where dad can fly in and pick up the meat."

Barb came around the bend in the trail and let out a gasp as she saw the three moose. About that time, we heard the engine on Earl's Cessna 180 droning over the trees. In a moment, he circled, wiggled his wings in recognition of our success and headed back to the lake. Barb and I hiked back to the snowmobiles and brought one up to Gerald. He was dressing out the bull with a razor sharp hand axe. We pitched in, holding the legs apart while he worked inside the body cavity. As we started on the second moose, Earl walked out of the woods on snowshoes.

"The plane is on the lake, but the lake is making slush," he said. "We've got to get these quarters skidded out as fast as possible."

Slush occurs when heavy snow presses down on lake ice, forcing water up through cracks. This creates a soft, sloppy layer between the ice and the unbroken snow above. Even in sub-zero temperatures, a layer of slush, from six inches to more than a foot, may exist for days. Snowmobiles mire down in it and ski planes can get stalled and subsequently frozen in as the temperature drops.

Earl grabbed the axe and took over dressing out the two cows while Gerald and I began skidding quarters to the plane. We roped each quarter to the back of the snowmobile, Gerald steering while I rode behind, alternately hopping off to push the quarters on steep uphills. We had a continual process going: Earl cutting with Barb's help, Gerald and I skidding the quarters to the lake. By late afternoon, we had all the quarters stacked by the plane and Earl flew one cow back with the guns. Gerald and Barb took the two snowmobiles back to the truck and I sat on the bloody quarters waiting for Earl's return for two more moose.

It was just getting dark when Earl came back for the last load, which consisted of the bull and me. He had taken the back and side seats out of the plane to make room for the four quarters. Bone weary, we loaded up the pieces of the bull and climbed into the cab. Earl was at the controls and I lay stretched out on top of the four quarters of moose, looking over my boots out the windshield. Muttering a few choice curses, Earl revved up the engine and began circling a side bay on the lake where slush had not yet appeared. He carved two turns sharply on one ski, then straightened out and headed down the lake. Almost immediately I could see a thick spray of slush flying off the skis and past the side window. Earl jammed the throttle to the firewall, trying for every ounce of acceleration.

As our speed increased, the far end of the lake rushed at us. Over my boots I fearfully watched the treeline coming as the engine raced and Earl held the nose down to get flying speed. About the time I found myself looking at rows of spruce trunks and expecting a big bang, he hauled back on the stick and we lifted off. Perhaps staggered off might be a better term. With the bull and I both on board, the Cessna was grossly overloaded and it wobbled into the air almost at stall speed. The last tense second we skimmed the treetops with a slight click, which I thought was a spruce branch or two popping the right ski. Through set teeth Earl muttered: "Come on, baby, come on!" fighting to keep us airborne, trying to coax one more mile an hour out of his struggling air-craft. We never did get more than 500 feet in the air, sort of groan-ing back with the overload. We dropped onto the ice at Crystal Lake, quickly taxied to the dock where the other moose carcasses were piled up, and climbed out.

"I didn't think we were going to make it," I said as we stacked the bull's quarters.

"Yeah, it was a bit tight," Earl admitted, then grinned and headed for the house.

Gerald and Barb drove up with the pickup truck and snowmo-biles. Together we went indoors for coffee and to get moose goo washed off. Earl came out of the bathroom wiping his face on a towel, another Molsons in his left hand. "Hey, I know where there's a Christmas party in Atikokan tonight!" he announced.

Gerald groaned. Barb groaned and I groaned. "I think I'll take a raincheck on that," I said. "Sleep is all I'm thinking about right now."

Earl laughed, put on his suit and left. Two things about Earl I'll never forget: He was one the nerviest pilots I ever met and also one of the most indestructible.

BY JACK HAUTALA

$\mathcal{T}$here were a lot of problems unique to winter flying; one of them involved keeping the engine running. On a day when the temperature was 30° or 40° below zero, the wind chill on a flying machine was sub-Arctic.

When we were doing a lot of teaching, students practiced landing with a dead engine. This was no big problem on the lake in warm weather since the student could simply shut off the engine, make the approach, flip on the ignition and the engine would catch. But in the winter, if an engine was completely shut off, it quite often would not start again. I told all the instructors to keep the power on in the winter even on landings. The only time a plane could be throttled back to idle was when the pilot was very sure he could make the runway.

When Al Beers was learning to fly, he was practicing emergency landings at 20° below zero over the ice on Burntside Lake. He came in, shut the power off, completed his approach, then attempted to kick the power back on and climb up. Unfortunately, the engine wouldn't restart. The plane hit a hard-packed snowmobile trail, flipped over on its back and suffered considerable damage.

Art Zorman was bringing his Citibra into a small lake in Canada where he had a cabin, cut the power and made a long glide. Seeing he was arriving short, he attempted to open it up but the engine had cooled off. He went into some trees and hit a cabin belonging to a neighbor. Art got out ok, but the plane and the cabin burned.

Other things could go wrong in winter. Quite a number of pilots around Ely flew 150-horsepower Champs, which had a bad habit of having the oil breather pipe that came out of the engine freeze shut. The trick with the Champ in the winter was to remove the breather pipe.

One winter day, Mike Weinzierl was heading for Harris Lake in his 150-horsepower Champ. A gusher of oil started hitting the windshield, obscuring his vision. When the breather pipe froze, the engine oil vapors were being forced out of the propeller seal. Wisely, Mike decided that since it was bitter cold, he would head back to Ely instead of going to Harris Lake. On the way back, the seal started to leak again, and he was forced to land and put in some more oil. Mike made it back to Ely, even with his windshield covered with oil.

An Otter in for winter repairs

THIS THING ABOUT ICE

BY BOB CARY

"*W*ant to go ice fishing up to Fourtown Lake tomorrow?"

It was early January, a crisp 30°-below-zero night and Pat Magie was on the line. "Sounds good," I said. "What's the deal?"

"Pete Czura and a pilot from the Cessna Company are flying in from Nebraska. Pete has an assignment to do a fly-in ice fishing article for *Field and Stream Magazine*. We've got a seat open in the plane."

"I'll fill it," I said. "What time?"

"Be at the seaplane base at 8 a.m."

Pete was an old fishing friend and fellow journalist from way back. "Hey, it'll be fun to fish a day with Pete."

The temperature had climbed slightly to only 25° below as we assembled on the ice in front of the Seaplane hangar at 8 o'clock. One thing about winter—it doesn't take a lot of tackle to go ice fishing. Couple of stubby rods, pocket box of hooks, ice auger, minnows and skimmer. And coffee. Nobody goes ice fishing without hot coffee.

In the winter, Magie's crew kept a couple of runways plowed on the surface of Shagawa Lake. This eliminated slush and made takeoffs and landings easy. Easy, that is, if the pilot followed the runway. If he came in crosswise to the runway it was like hitting a deep ditch and would result in the landing gear being sheared off. The Cessna pilot had landed a 185 wheel plane on the east-west plowed runway. It was tied down near the hangar.

As four of us piled our fishing gear into Magie's ski-equipped Cessna 180, a yellow sun peeked through frosty haze over the surrounding woods. As we roared into the sky, the forest below, decorated with last night's frost, stretched in a pale lavender panorama below the plane's skis. Fourtown was over a few hills and valleys

163

from the base, perhaps a 15 minute hop at most. We skimmed in smoothly and unloaded our tackle. Pete persuaded Magie to shoot a few landings in the Cessna so he could get photos for the magazine article. The Cessna company pilot and I drilled holes and put out lines baited with wiggling minnows.

Pat Magie talks over a trip with a client

It looked like Pete was going to score on a nice article because the walleyes and northern pike began cooperating with enthusiasm. By noon, we had eight fish on the ice, drank some coffee and assessed the situation.

"We'll need to pull out in a few minutes," Magie announced. "Weather's changing."

The sun was still bright. The day warming up quite well and the fish were biting. What was this stuff with the weather? We went back to our lines and were busy with some more fish when Magie said: "OK, that's it, guys. Time to head back."

He was looking at a line of clouds forming on the southern horizon, a somewhat unusual pattern for northern Minnesota. We seldom get any weather from the south and this one didn't look threatening.

Pete glanced to the south and shrugged. "Hey, the fish are hitting and I'm getting a great story. Let's keep it going."

"No way. We've got to get out of here." Magie headed for the plane with the ice auger and his tackle.

"Reel up guys," I said. "Time to get going."

"Doesn't look like anything bad to me," the Cessna pilot opined.

"Look," I said, "if Magie says we get out of here, then we get out of here."

There was a lot of grumbling as Pete and the Cessna pilot gathered up their tackle, bagged the fish and climbed back into the plane, but the front was coming in a hurry. The sun was gone, and the first wisps of gray cloud were already overhead.

Magie flipped the ignition, we bumped over the snow, gathered speed and were airborne. I was sitting in the co-pilot seat, the company pilot and Pete in the rear. As we angled up through the thick mist, I was alarmed to see a rapid build-up of white ice on the leading edge of the wing directly overhead. Magie muttered something and aimed the nose down sharply, leveling off just over the cattails in a long snowbound marsh.

"Warmer down here," he explained. Must have been. The ice came off the wing, but the windshield was wet. We hurtled through the gathering gloom, down creeks, across small lakes and through spruce narrows that barely accommodated the aircraft. I was frankly terrified. I knew we were approaching Ely but we had one more high ridge to cross from the valley in which we were flying to Shagawa Lake and the seaplane base. Before I had much time to dwell on that, Magie banked hard left, jammed the throttle to the wall and we followed the ice-laden trees up the ridge. There was not a sound from the two passengers in the back as the ice built up again on the leading edge of the wing. We came over the crest and started our glide to the lake surface, but the controls were sluggish and we couldn't make the mile over to the hangar. Instead, we came down hard on the skis, thumped and bumped over snow ridges and snowmobile tracks as the ice flew off in plate-size hunks.

At the base, Magie cut the power and we climbed out. Pete and the company pilot hit the snow running and disappeared in the direction of the radio shack where the ice fridge held a couple of cold six packs of beer.

As Magie and I were emptying out the plane I pointed at the soggy sky: "Kinda scary up there."

"How's that?"

"How long can a plane stay in the air with that ice building

165

up?"

Magie rubbed a glove over his face. "You've got about thirty seconds when the ice builds up to where the plane quits flying."

"Sheesh," I said. "That's pretty tight."

"Oh, no. I've flown over that ridge a thousand times. It takes only twenty seconds to clear it. We had ten seconds extra any way you want to figure."

UNLUCKY *on* SKIS, LUCKY *in* LOVE BY BOB CARY

*W*hen Jesse Swanson was doing a considerable amount of flying around Ely, he was also courting a young woman who lived with her mother in a fine house on Burntside Lake. One winter day, Jesse and Louis Palcher flew over to Burntside intending to put on a show and impress the women. After a couple of loops and slow rolls over the roof of the house, Jesse stalled the aircraft and smacked the ice right in front of the house. The plane was a total wreck, but Jesse and Louis had the good luck to walk away unhurt. Their good luck continued. Jesse went on to marry the daughter, and Louis eventually married the mother and moved into that nice big house.

Hunters flying out

SNOWSHOE TROUBLE

BY BOB CARY

$\mathcal{L}$ee Schumacher served in the U.S. Air Force in England, which is where he met his wife Muff who is an integral part of this story. Lee later studied to be a pharmacist and went to work for druggist George Bertola at the James Drug Co. Store in Ely. Bertola had been a flier in World War II and like a lot of local folk, had his own floatplane. Schumacher checked out on floats and flew for Pat Magie at Wilderness Wings. He and his wife eventually bought out Bertola and took over operation of the James Drug Co. Store in Ely, but he kept up his part-time flying.

One January day, pilot Wiley Gregg, Lou Ann Cherne and Lou Ann's two dogs set out on a snowshoe trek from Big Moose Lake to Burntside Lake. Pat Magie flew them to Big Moose in a Cessna 180 on skis, dropped them off and went back to Ely, expecting them to phone for a pickup later. They might have had an enjoyable hike except the lakes were full of slush. This phenomenon occurs in the north country when extra heavy snowfall presses down on the ice, forcing water up through cracks, creating a layer of wet slop that is insulated from the cold by a top layer of soft snow. There is no warning. It is not visible until a person walks into it.

In any event, Wiley and Lou Ann eventually ran into slush. When they took a step, each snowshoe came out of the slush and hit the frigid air creating a ball of ice. In short order they were each dragging 25 pounds of ice on each foot. They stopped numerous times on dry snow to beat the ice off, but it was only a temporary remedy. As they kept walking, they kept running into slush, which slowed their progress measurably. By dark they were only halfway to their destination, but no one in Ely knew this.

When darkness fell and no phone call came to the seaplane

base, Pat Magie grew increasingly worried. The northwoods is no place to spend a night in the middle of winter without a camping outfit and a good sleeping bag, something Magie knew neither Wiley nor Lou Ann possessed. He phoned Lee Schumacher and outlined the problem, asking Lee if he would fly out with him to try and find the missing snowshoers, figuring two sets of eyes were better than one.

Lee Schumacher

They took off from Shagawa Lake in the dark in Magie's Cessna, flying little more than 100 feet over the treetops in their search. A circle of Big Moose, Cummings and Crab Lake on the snowshoe route to Burntside Lake revealed nothing but trees, snow and darkness. Now growing worried, Magie landed at the Crab Lake portage from where the two pilots continued their search on snowshoes in the dark, hoping to cross the trail of the missing hikers. Finally, they spotted the glow of a small fire on the northeast side of Crab Lake and located Wiley, Lou Ann and the two dogs, intact but extremely tired from their ordeal. Recognizing that the hikers could go no further, Magie snowshoed back to the plane, started the engine, taxied across the snow and loaded in Lou Ann and the dogs. He had Lee and Wiley push on the wings to get the plane rolling over the slush and finally took off, heading for Ely with his cargo.

Lee knew where Marian Dietrich's cabin was located near the

portage into Burntside Lake and persuaded Wiley to hike in that direction seeking shelter in case Magie couldn't get back. Wiley was almost totally bushed from plodding through slush all day and kept wanting to stop and rest. Eventually, they heard Magie's plane returning. Lee had a railroad flare in his jacket pocket, pulled it out and ignited it to signal the pilot where to land. Magie came in and immediately hit slush. Fearing to get bogged down and the skis frozen in, he taxied past the two men, yanked the door of the plane open and shouted for them to run and jump on the skis while he kept the plane moving. "I'm not stopping!" he yelled at the two men.

In spite of his fatigue, Wiley sprinted with Lee to the moving aircraft, and they scrambled onto the skis, eventually climbing inside the cab as Magie got the ship airborne. They finally made it back to the plowed runway on the ice at the Shagawa Lake airbase, landed and called it a night. Mission accomplished.

Well, almost.

It was very late at night when Lee got home and he didn't want to wake up Muff to tell her where he had been, preferring to wait until morning. As it turned out, he rushed off to the drug store in the morning so Muff did not know what had occurred the previous night.

About noon, a delivery truck arrived from the florist shop in Ely with a box for Lee. Although mystified, Muff accepted the box from the driver and opened it. Inside the box were a dozen red roses and a note reading simply: "Thanks for what you did for me last night." It was signed: "Lou Ann."

Lee had a lot of fast explaining to do when he came home that night from the drug store.

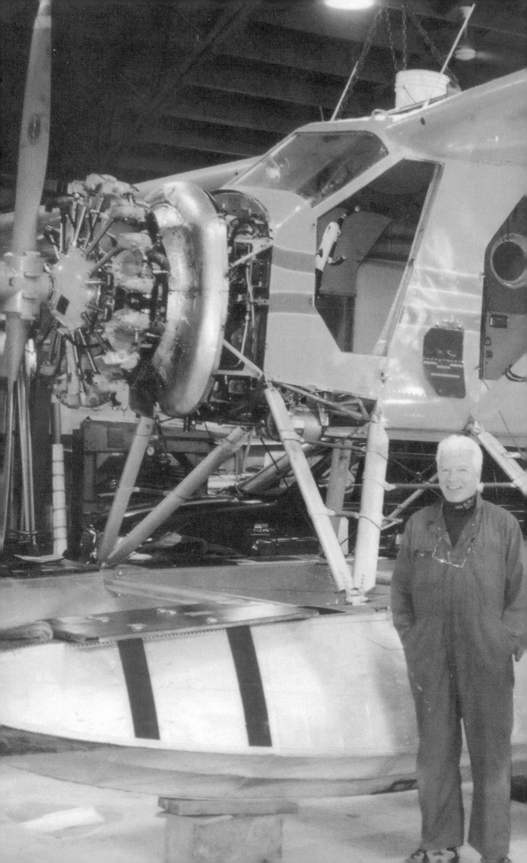

A BYGONE ERA

"*Once we were privileged to be a small part of that glorious era with its wonderful floatplane fliers.*"

THE WAR *of* '78

BY BOB CARY

*A*nybody who has been a newspaper reporter for any length of time develops a mental smoke detector that starts buzzing when somebody is trying to blow a little smoke. Thus, when a sharp-eyed individual came into the newspaper office and started asking a lot of questions about the Boundary Waters Canoe Area, the smoke detector buzzed.

It was 1978. There was legislation up before the U.S. Congress to redo the 1964 Wilderness Act which created the Boundary Waters. The new laws would eliminate the last floatplane service at Ely—Pat Magie's Wilderness Wings Airways.

Flights into the wilderness had long been banned by federal law. The reason was that the burgeoning fleet of floatplanes were flying into the back country, hauling in fishermen in minutes to lakes that took canoe paddlers days to reach. In addition, there had been 40 remote resorts serviced by floatplanes which created considerable traffic. The fly-ins ended and the resorts were bought out by the government. The wilderness interior became floatplane free, other than U.S. Forest Service patrol craft. Magie had the only flying service remaining in operation. He flew canoe paddlers to a half dozen lakes outside the wilderness from where they could paddle and portage into the wilderness and canoe back to their starting point.

Even this reduced use irritated some of the wilderness advocates. The 1978 law simply expanded the perimeter of the BWCA and eliminated any lakes Magie could fly into. There were a lot of writers visiting the Ely area in1978, nearly all of them in support of expanding the wilderness. Just about all of them came in, identified themselves and gathered their information. But now and then, one showed up trying to act like a tourist.

Thus, when a sharp-eyed stranger arrived at the newspaper asking a lot of questions, the smoke detector went off.

"Who are you writing for?" he was asked.

The stranger, who had not identified himself, countered with: "What makes you think I'm writing for somebody?"

"The questions. Only a reporter would ask those kinds of questions."

"Well, if you must know, I'm writing an article for Outside Magazine. I'm up here with Jack Ford."

Everyone in Ely was aware that the son of former President Gerald Ford was in the area on a canoe trip to help boost the latest law changes.

"Where did you and Jack Ford go on your canoe trip?" the writer was asked.

"We went from Fourtown Lake to Horse Lake, down the Horse River to the Basswood River and back through Basswood Lake," he said proudly.

Remote Fourtown Lake was one of the perimeter lakes the proposed legislation was designed to eliminate as a fly-in designation. "How did you get to Fourtown Lake?" the reporter was asked. "You surely didn't paddle up there. You flew in, didn't you?"

The reporter looked uncomfortable, somewhat angry, perhaps feeling he had said too much. "We went in by hang glider," he said with a smirk. "We had a special dispensation from the Pope."

"Boy, you are sure cute. I bet you flew in with Pat Magie and you're writing a story aimed at eliminating Magie's fly-in service."

The reporter let out a snort and shot out the door.

About fifteen minutes went by and who walked in but Jack Ford, the president's son. He shook hands and introduced himself, although we had no trouble recognizing him. "I hear you had a run-in with the writer who is with me," he said.

"He tried to B.S. his way around the newspaper and it just doesn't go here," we explained.

Ford pulled up a chair and sat down. "What was the problem?"

"The problem is that you two started a canoe trip from an area where you flew in and it's an access that the legislation you support would eliminate along with the pilot who flew you in. My bet is that the story won't mention the fact that you flew in. The story will be all about how you paddled into the wilderness."

"Well, we did paddle."

"Yeah, after you flew in. Did you tell the pilot you were doing a story to knock him out of business? Why didn't you paddle and portage a couple of extra days to get to Fourtown and then start your trip?"

"We had time constraints. We were on a tight schedule."

"Everybody's on a tight schedule. Why should you be different?"

Ford laughed and got up. "Yeah, I can see how it looks, kind of hypocritical. I guess if I lived up here I would probably think like you people do."

"Look, if someone doesn't like floatplanes, that's their business but we don't like the idea of using a floatplane to do a paddle-only wilderness story."

Ford laughed some more, shook his head and walked out. When the story appeared in the magazine, just like we thought, no mention was made of either the floatplane or something else we found out. When Jack Ford and the magazine writer arrived at the Upper Falls of the Basswood River, nearing the end of their trip, they were met by a motor launch from an outfitter and transported the last 25 miles back to the highway, saving another day's paddling. The launch service to Basswood Falls was another item the proposed '78 legislation was designed to eliminate.

One more thing. When they got to Basswood Falls, it was pouring rain so they couldn't get the photos the reporter wanted of Ford carrying his canoe across the portage. A day or so later, when the rain quit, they took the launch 25 miles back up to the falls, canoe and all, shot the photos of Jack Ford making the portage and then took the launch 25 miles back to civilization. So much for the paddle trip. However, the magazine article was quite a hit and no doubt contributed to public and congressional support for the legislation because Congress passed the Boundary Waters Canoe Area Wilderness Act in 1978 that put Magie and the remaining commercial bush pilots out of business and also eliminated motor launch service to Basswood Falls.

Along with the fliers, there were lots of local folk along the border who were pretty irate about the whole business, but from the standpoint of the bush pilots themselves, it was the best thing that happened to them. Even with a Cessna dealership, his floatplane flying school and wilderness fly-ins, Magie had a heck of a time trying to make ends meet. He was always in trouble trying to

176

meet bank payments, take care of the payroll and buy new parts and floats for his aircraft. He operated for years on the edge of insolvency. When the fliers were legislated out of business at Ely, they flew to Alaska and started over. At least the serious ones like Magie and Kenny Bellows. Up there they found millions of acres of forests teeming with wildlife, lakes and rivers full of salmon, trout and grayling. All of this in a vast area with hardly any roads where the only way to get around is by boat or by floatplane. It is a bush pilot's heaven.

In Alaska, Pat Magie not only established a thriving flying service at Cordova but also came to own a number of outpost fishing and hunting camps plus a houseboat fleet on Prince William Sound. He became more successful than he had ever dreamed. Kenny Bellows hit it big with his Bell Air operation in Sitka and is well-to-do even by Alaskan standards.

And they are still doing what they love most—flying the bush.

Loading up for a trip

BUSH PILOTS' LAST STAND
BY BOB CARY

*R*ob Howden looks like a bush pilot. At least how you might think a veteran pilot should look. His silver mane of hair caps square shoulders, a square jaw and a steely gaze, one that has intently studied thousands of square miles of Canadian bush from the Ontario-Minnesota line to the top of the Arctic.

Rob grew up at Campbell's Cabins and Lac La Croix Quetico Air Services on the Canadian side of Lac La Croix. His dad, Dr. Lorri Howden, a physician in Winnipeg, worked at the lodge part time in the summer. He married Marjorie Campbell, one of two daughters of the lodge owner. Young Rob first came to the resort in 1942, less than a year old, in a toilet paper carton for a cradle. When Rob was big enough to run a boat and motor, he began working as a fishing guide. His cousin Jay Handberg, whose dad Bob, married the other Campbell sister, Isabelle, grew up at the resort becoming business manager.

Rob had an early interest in the floatplanes flying in and out of the remote resort, accessible only by air or by boat shuttle. He completed his pilot training in the 1960s, eventually becoming chief pilot overseeing a fleet of planes that currently includes an Otter, two Beavers, two Cessnas and a Champ. There is history behind some of the planes. The Otter, C-FNFI, in operation since 1960, spent much of its life in the Canadian Arctic before being acquired by Lac La Croix Quetico. Beaver C-FHAN was built in 1952 for service in South America, eventually worked its way North and came to Ontario by way of Ely, Minnesota. Beaver C-GDZD was built in 1952 for the U.S. military, traveled to Japan, back to Arizona, north to Alberta, and farther north to the James Bay area on the edge of the Arctic. It became part of the La Croix fleet in 1980.

The present six ships comprise the main floatplane flight service operating on the Minnesota-Ontario border today, providing a type of fly-in that is rapidly vanishing.

Leithold Seaplane Service ad; Unloading at camp

"The North Country floatplane territory is shrinking every year," says Howden. "Most of the back country flying is now to public or private fields that accommodate wheel planes. We happen to be located in an unique area where floatplanes are still a necessity."

This includes flying canoes, gear and people for over 30 U.S. canoe outfitters who schedule trips to lakes in the roadless wilderness from which they can paddle back to the home base or to another lake to be picked up for the return flight. Also, hundreds of flights are made to Canadian resorts and outpost fishing and hunting camps.

Jay Handberg maintains close relations with the Lac La Croix First Nation band of Ojibwe, which has a large reservation a few miles east of the seaplane base. The Ojibwe village provides a roster of skilled fishing and canoe guides for the resort guests. Also, under treaty provisions, the Ontario government has set aside 20 lakes within adjacent Quetico Provincial Park for exclusive motor use by Native American guides. Handberg's planes make daily runs to these lakes providing a high quality angling experience.

In addition to his flying, Howden operates a thriving trading post adjacent to the Canadian customs station on Sandpoint Lake, main entry point for fishing boats and floatplanes heading to La Croix and farther north. His home is near the post, which means each day he commutes to work by floatplane from Sandpoint to the main base on La Croix.

Rob Howden with a Beaver at Lac La Croix

"I never wake up in the morning without thinking about how much I love my work," he says. "And each day I take off toward the east with a hot cup of coffee in one hand watching the splendor as the sun comes up over the forest rim."

In more than 25,000 hours of air time, Howden has never had a pile-up, testimony to his skill and careful eye to detail. "Every summer we have from six to nine pilots training and flying. I impress on them the importance of taking care of details, of checking the gas tanks, making sure the controls are operating correctly and the load properly adjusted. When they take off, they are paying close attention to wind, weather and the area they are flying over. They are aware of what options are available for landing in case of an emergency."

Howden says when he is traveling over the forest, he never simply flies along like a tourist. "I continually scan the terrain ahead and below, noting locations of lakes that might offer a landing site if an engine stopped, where there are sand beaches and remote cabins useful for emergency shelter. All of these items I log into my memory bank for possible future use."

There is even backlog information on what to do if forced down in the trees.

"Pilots have been killed in crashes, not from the front impact," notes Howden, "but from cargo coming forward in the cab and smashing them in the back. Old timers say to pick out a big tree in the woods and at the last minute, hook it with a wing so it spins the plane sideways in the crash. This causes the cargo to break out through the side of the plane instead of shooting forward into the pilot seat."

He notes that all mental map information is of utmost importance on flights to the far north, to Fort Severn and similar fishing and hunting areas near Hudson Bay. He has memorized the main fuel stops and remote fuel caches where a plane may drop in during an emergency.

"The pilot simply has to know all these things. There is no time to look this information up with an emergency at hand."

He insists some of the most demanding flying has been during forest fires—getting crews and supplies close to the burning area. "We have transported all kinds of equipment, even including a tractor once that was taken apart so we could fly the pieces in to a project.

"There are not a lot of old bush pilots left flying now," he laments. "Roads compete. Government regulations and steep insurance rates have boosted the cost of using floatplanes. Young pilots now are much more interested in getting time on wheel planes because that's where the jobs and the future lie."

As he approaches his 60th birthday, Rob Howden has begun contemplating his eventual retirement from commercial flying. After over 25,000 hours of air time he has come to realize the years are catching up with him and that, incredibly, he has become one of the pilots the young fliers talk about—an old-timer, one of the legends of bush plane flying.

Howden, like every one of the pilots we talked to for this book, would not have traded his experiences for any other type of life. They are an incredible fraternity, these fliers, who will eventually become names on yellowing flight sheets in some dusty filing cabinet; faces that fade with memory.

There were many more we never got to talk with, fliers like Rusty Meyers and Verne Jones. Doug Bohman, Dave Hangartner, the Lamms and Francis Einerson.

The ones we wrote about were the careful and the daring, the flamboyant, the pragmatic, the lucky and the very unlucky. They are vanishing into history now along with those of us who knew of them or flew with them. Environmentally aware visitors to the northland today look out upon the vast expanse of green forest, glimmering lakes and blue sky with a sense of reverence, a feeling of awe. We old-timers have that same sense, that same feeling, but we also hear, sometimes only in memory, the distinct distant hum of a small aircraft, sunlight glinting in a momentary flash of silver off a set of aluminum pontoons high in the air. Once we were privileged to be a small part of that glorious era with its wonderful floatplane fliers.

This is who they were. Who they are. The old and the bold.

"JACKPINE BOB" CARY

*A*uthor Bob Cary, known across the Northland as Jackpine Bob, was born in Joliet, Illinois, on October 20, 1921. He was raised in the farm country, attended public schools, and had finished Community College when WWII broke out. He enlisted in the U.S. Marines and served in combat from 1942 to 1945 with the 2nd Division. He returned to civilian life and attended the Chicago Academy of Fine Art for two years, then went to work as a writer and illustrator. Bob worked for the *Joliet Herald-News*, *Joliet Spectator*, and as outdoor editor of the *Chicago Daily News* and the *Ely Echo*. Jackpine Bob currently is a columnist at the *Mesabi Daily News*. He has seven books in print and countless magazine articles published. He has illustrated both his own and other authors' books, and owns an art gallery in Ely. Bob owned and operated a canoe outfitting and guiding service for eight years at Ely, and over the last 60 years has flown with many of the most noted bush pilots in North America, including co-author Jack Hautala of Ely.

"Jackpine Bob" Cary

JACK HAUTALA

$\ell$was born on May 25, 1934, and had my first plane ride with my dad, Ernie Hautala, in a Curtiss Robin in Tower, Minnesota, when I was three years old. I attended public schools in Soudan and Ely, then worked one winter on a copper nickel survey at the Kawishiwi River site. I started to work for Winton Hydroelectric Station on maintenance and ended as superintendent 41 years later. The job provided a lot of extra time to fly.

I started flying with Millard Whittig in 1955 but was drafted into the Army, where I served from 1956 to 1958. I had an Army friend named Dale Kattraba who was a flier and provided some dual instruction in a J-3 Cub. I also flew some in a Piper Tri Pacer. After Army duty, I returned to my job at Winton, got married in 1959, divorced in 1962 and went back to flying. I earned my private pilot license with Ray Morse at the Ely Airport in 1964.

I bought a J-3 Cub on floats at Eveleth for $1600 in 1965, then a 90-horsepower Champ. I got a commercial license in 1967, instrument rating in 1969, and multi-engine seaplane rating in a Beech 18 in 1970. I obtained an airplane multi-engine land rating in an Aero Commander 500 in Minneapolis in 1975, and a Chief Instrument Flight Instructor rating in the same plane in 1976.

From 1967 until Pat Magie went out of business a decade later, my brother Wiley and I flew Minnesota, Canada, Alaska and the Arctic. I also taught a lot of pilots to fly instruments. It was the greatest time of my life. I bought a Cessna 185 in 1980. In 1989, I could no longer pass the flight physical and sold my Cessna. Over the years, I compiled a great amount of information on the Ely area seaplane days, a fabulous era that is included in this book.

Jack Hautala

Grab a cup of coffee, pull a chair up to the table, and listen in on a story-swapping session with some living legends of the bush pilot era.

BOB CARY

"Jackpine Bob" Cary has never flown a floatplane himself, but knows and has flown with many of North America's most noted bush pilots, and has been on a number of wild rides. During the eight years when he owned Canadian Border Outfitters, he worked with Pat Magie's Wilderness Wings to fly many of his clients into the roadless expanse of northern Minnesota and Canada. Bob has lived in Ely with his wife Edith for about 40 years and witnessed the heyday of bush pilots in northern Minnesota.

JACK HAUTALA

Co-author Jack Hautala has lived in Ely his whole life. Jack began flying lessons with Millard Whittig in 1955, but the first flight he took was with his dad, Ernie Hautala, who was one of the first bush pilots in the area. Jack's brother, Wiley, was also an accomplished bush pilot. During his flying career, Jack flew for Pat Magie and owned a bunch of planes himself. He did a lot of flying up to Canada and Alaska and even in the Arctic. He also taught a number of other pilots how to fly instruments. When he was done flying, he sold airplanes.

MILT NELSON

Milt flew and barnstormed around the Duluth area for ten years before taking a job with the U.S. Forest Service in Ely. He flew for the Forest Service for twenty years, from 1942 to 1962, working with other legendary bush pilots like Chick Beel and Walt Newman. After the Forest Service job, Milt flew for an additional ten years before retiring from flying. He and Walt still go down to the Forest Service hangar to talk shop.

WALT NEWMAN

After his three and a half years in the Navy, Walt took flying lessons with Leithold Aviation and learned to fly at Sandy Point. After he'd earned his private, seaplane and commercial ratings, he flew for Leithold Aviation for nine years and went with them to Wisconsin once the air ban came into effect in northern Minnesota. In 1957, he returned to Ely and worked for the U.S. Forest Service for twenty years.

TOM DAYTON

Tom got his wings in late '70. After the Vietnam War, he worked in intelligence for a short time. He earned his floatplane rating from Pat Magie and flew people around on sightseeing trips in the Ely area for about a year. Then he connected with Kenny Bellows, who got him a job in Alaska. Tom spent a number of years flying the bush in Alaska, including one summer spent with the Forest Service in the southeastern panhandle. After a short break in Colorado, he is back up in Alaska, flying the bush.

BOB HODGE

Through the CPT program, Bob earned a number of ratings, including his instructor rating, and then taught students with Millard Whittig until World War II. During the war, he was part of the Air Force and flew litter patients in the South Pacific. After the war, he started his own flight school with two other pilots. In 1950, he became part of the DNR and was stationed in Ely until 1976. He then took a DNR position in St. Paul, and was eventually promoted to assistant director of enforcement and chief pilot.

WAYNE ERICKSON

Wayne grew up around airplanes; his dad flew in World War II, and his uncles flew the bush around Rainy Lake with the Bohman brothers. Wayne worked for the Bohmans for a couple of years, and then went up to Alaska where he flew charters, mail runs and hunters and fishermen. He also flew out of northern Greenland for a few years, servicing a scientific research outfit on the icepack. In 1989, Wayne took the Forest Service job in Ely and has been there since.

PAT LOE

At St. Cloud State, Pat accumulated all his ratings and instructed for a few years. After flying for commuter airlines for a time, he tired of the routine, took a leave of absence and went to Alaska and flew the bush for a fishing and hunting operation for three years. In 1998, a job opened up at the Forest Service base in Ely, and Pat joined on at that time, returning to his home town.

CD INDEX:

1. Introduction . . . . .Bob Cary

2. Meet the Gang . . . . .all

3. Hodge & the Ice Fishermen . . . . .Bob Cary

4. Canoe Party at Big Moose . . . . .Jack Hautala

5. Lunchtime Airways . . . . .Bob Hodge

6. Flying Backward . . . . .Walt Newman

7. Landing a Plane in the Woods . . . . .Milt Nelson

8. The Champ Stalls Out . . . . .Jack Hautala

9. Getting Out of Goat Lake . . . . .Tom Dayton

10. Broken Prop . . . . .Walt Newman

11. Netting Busy . . . . .Bob Hodge

12. We're High Enough . . . . .Tom Dayton

13. The VIP Lineup . . . . .Milt Nelson

14. The Goat Hunters . . . . .Tom Dayton

15. Hitting Ground . . . . .Jack Hautala

16. Lightning Strikes . . . . .Walt Newman

17. Beaver Dam Rescue . . . . .Bob Hodge

18. Ashes . . . . .Milt Nelson

19. Magie & the Ice Storm .Bob Cary

20. Meet Two Current Forest Service Pilots . . . . .Bob Cary

21. The Blowdown of 1999,
    Fires and Bush Flying . . . . . . .Wayne Erickson and Pat Loe